Snow in August

Gao Xingjian

Translated by Gilbert C. F. Fong

The Chinese University Press

Snow in August
By Gao Xingjian
Translated by Gilbert C. F. Fong

© Gao Xingjian, 2000, 2001
English language translation © Gilbert C. F. Fong, 2003

First published in Chinese as *Bayue xue* by Lianjing Chubanshe,
Taiwan, 2000
Revised edition published in *Gao Xingjian juzuo xuan* by
Ming Pao Press, Hong Kong, 2001
First published in English by The Chinese University Press,
Hong Kong, 2003
First English paperback edition, 2004

ISBN 962–996–101–6

THE CHINESE UNIVERSITY PRESS
The Chinese University of Hong Kong
Sha Tin, N. T., Hong Kong
Fax: +852 2603 6692
     +852 2603 7355
E-mail: cup@cuhk.edu.hk
Web-site: www.chineseupress.com

Photographs courtesy of National Taiwan Junior College of Performing
Arts 國立臺灣戲曲專科學校. Photographer: Ming-hsun Lee 李銘訓

Paintings courtesy of Gao Xingjian

Printed in Hong Kong

Contents

Introduction:
Marginality, Zen, and
Omnipotent Theatre

I want to pass on to the Beijing opera actors the knowledge and experience
gained from my work in experimental drama in the West.... My aim is to
create a modern musical theatre based on the foundations of Eastern
traditional drama, an omnipotent theatre of singing, dialogue, movement,
and the martial arts.

— *Gao Xingjian on* Snow in August *(Gao 2002: 6)*

Snow in August is based on the life of Huineng (633–713), the Sixth Patriarch
of Zen Buddhism and founder of the Sudden Enlightenment School.
According to Gao Xingjian, the sources for this "major drama about life"
are Huineng's autobiographical Platform Sutra 壇經[1] and various *koan* cases
(Gao 2002: 5). It is not surprising that Gao Xingjian has discovered a kindred
spirit in Huineng, as there are elements in the Zen master's life that strike
a chord with our playwright. To put it more succinctly, Huineng, like Gao
Xingjian, was always someone on the margins of society, often by choice.
According to Huineng's biographies (which are half legend and half
history), he was an impoverished woodcutter from the southern part of
China, the backwater of Chinese culture. (In the play, Huineng is first
referred to as "the barbarian from the south.") He never had any schooling,
but despite being illiterate, he had an uncanny ability to understand difficult
Buddhist sutras and elucidate Buddhist tenets in a straightforward manner.
He was an outsider to the religious order — he did not belong to any temple,
and he was not even an ordained monk when he became the Sixth Patriarch.

Like our playwright, Huineng lived in exile many times during his life. When he was young, his father, who had been an official in the capital, lost his post and was banished to live in Canton in the south with his family. After Huineng was chosen as patriarch, he was forced to flee from the temple to live among hunters in the mountains to avoid persecution from jealous monks. He shied away from the seat of power, spurning the Emperor and the Empress Dowager's royal summons to serve in the capital as "Teacher of Heaven and Men." This was of course a grand gesture on his part, an attempt to underline his refusal to become a figurehead of state orthodoxy.

Some scholars have noticed that there is a latent anti-establishment stance in Zen Buddhist beliefs. Huineng's famous *gatha* poem, which is quoted in the play, alludes to his non-conformist attitude:

> The *bodhi* is not a tree,
> Nor the mind a mirror bright;
> Buddha nature is always pure,
> Where can any dust alight?

While orthodox Buddhist masters typically insisted on cultivating virtues and doing good works to achieve enlightenment, Huineng, on the other hand, endorsed the idea of enlightenment through a direct understanding of one's self-nature. *Bodhi* is wisdom and, according to Huineng, it cannot be grown or cultivated — he was to assert later that *Bodhi* comes as "sudden enlightenment," thus the name of his school of Zen Buddhsim. The mind cannot be objectified as a mirror, as Buddha nature is self-nature — it resides within oneself, not in extraneous icons or deeds, which are but delusions. It is also pure and empty, such that even dust can find no place to settle, let alone soil it. In contrast, Shenxiu, the senior instructor and foil to Huineng in almost every aspect (in Huineng's biography and in the play), still clings to objects in his metaphorizing *Bodhi* and the mind:

> The body is a *Bodhi* tree,
> The mind a mirror bright,
> Always wipe it clean,
> And let no dust alight.

Shenxiu is firmly rooted in the orthodoxy and its tenets. To him, good works and the cultivation of virtues ("Always wipe it clean") will lead to the "way." In contrast, Huineng's "no-mind" approach moves beyond orthodoxy and abandons all attachments to enter into the realm of the void, thus achieving the highest pinnacle of enlightenment. This approach proves to be far superior, and he ultimately wins the succession to the patriarchate. His *Platform Sutra* is the only Buddhist sutra (*jing* 經) written by a Chinese master (all others were written by Indian masters). Historically, he was credited with revolutionizing Buddhism in China by giving it Chinese characteristics and effectively transforming it into a Chinese school of thought.

The episodes of Huineng's life are highlighted in *Snow in August*, as if Gao Xingjian had found the "objective correlative" for his ideal personality, the perfect vehicle for his worldview and philosophy of life — *indépendance totale* and freedom. As Gao Xingjian echoes Huineng: "You could say that there is Chan [Zen] in every person, and everyone can become a bodhisattva." (Chang 2002a: 15) The *truth*, then, is not attached to any one thing, and it depends on no one but the individual himself or herself; in other words, it is contingent upon the actualization of individualism in its ultimate form. The significance of Huineng, according to Gao, does not reside in his status as a revered religious leader, but in his inherent understanding of the truth about human existence and salvation, which represents a major breakthrough and "freeing up" of religion:

> First, he [Huineng] broke through the obsession with material objects. He didn't even want the traditional cassock and bowl but preferred to just try to achieve a spiritual connection or tacit understanding between master and acolyte....
>
> Secondly, Huineng was unwilling to play the role of a messiah. He only guided people and inspired them to realize their own natures.... He has an even more modern image than Jesus Christ. Christ sacrificed himself to save others, but the thought of Huineng is even more modern — the point is not who will save who, but to go out and save yourself! (Chang 2002a: 13)

Liu Zaifu, a famous scholar and good friend of Gao Xingjian, once commented in a lecture that Gao's work could be summarized in one word: self-salvation. In *Snow in August*, Gao tries to tackle the universal problem of freeing oneself from life's sufferings, and Zen represents a supreme transcendence of worldly troubles and privations (Gao 2002: 5).

In *Snow in August*, Huineng is portrayed as a thinker, and that, Gao insists, is the only way he could be presented in drama — if drama were used to promote religion, it would become a meaningless endeavour (Chang 2002a: 14). Gao Xingjian does not wish to promote Zen Buddhism — while he appreciates its scepticism towards language, he does not find it agreeable as a religious practice (Gao 1992a: 114). On many occasions, both public and private, Gao has said that he is not a believer and warned against regarding his plays as treatises on Zen Buddhism or any other philosophy (Gao 1992b: 136). However, there is no denying that a Zen ambience pervades many of his stories and plays — some critics even go as far as to insist that Gao is the creator of a kind of Zen theatre (Zhao 1999). Even Gao himself claims that with *Snow in August*, it is the first time in Chinese drama that Zen has been successfully integrated into a play, unlike many previous attempts which merely recount in a straightforward manner the stories of retribution and virtue rewarded (Chang 2002a: 13–14).

> The ultimate goal of theatre is to express human nature.... This play should have a spiritual impact on people; it will be a jolt to the innermost mind, so it requires a powerful theatrical form. So long as you grasp the essence of Chan [Zen], you can move the audience. (Chang 2002a: 15)

What does Gao mean when he says that the play requires "a powerful theatrical form"? The 2002 production of *Snow in August* in Taipei, directed by Gao Xingjian himself, was an extravaganza. It featured fifty actors and actresses, a chorus of fifty, four percussionists, and a symphony orchestra made up of ninety musicians for a total of two hundred-odd performers. The impact came not only from the number but also from the onset of sights and sounds on the stage, a theatre of "singing, dialogue, movement and the martial arts." The aim was to create a modern musical form based on Beijing opera, an all encompassing theatre which Gao called "omnipotent theatre" 全能的戲劇.

The Taipei production of *Snow in August* aspired to expand the possibilities of theatrical performance, in particular, Beijing opera. There had been many attempts to modernize the traditional art form, but they were all hampered by the preoccupation that the end product, no matter the experimentation, would still be Beijing opera. Gao Xingjian was different: he wanted total independence in order to free himself from all constraints. He started from zero and would be willing to accept any result as long as it was innovative — "it [*Snow in August*] includes everything, but is not any one thing," (Chang 2002a: 11) i.e., it was not anything in the repertoire of existent theatrical forms.

In this "omnipotent theatre," the actors also had to be "omnipotent actors" 全能的演員. They were required to sing, dance, and perform in different theatrical styles, and be accomplished in many performing arts techniques, both Chinese and Western. The performance was to be different from Beijing opera and stage plays, and the directing and acting had to be founded on a new understanding of contemporary theatre, i.e., what Gao Xingjian calls the "tripartite actor" — the actor, entering into a state of neutrality, should be able to separate himself from the character to display his art to the audience in a self-conscious and interesting manner (Gao 2002: 5; Fong 1999: xviii–xxi).

"Omnipotent theatre" developed out of the concept of "total theatre," which Gao first advocated in 1984 with the experimental *Wild Man* (*Yeren* 野人). The play was an attempt to return modern drama to the traditional concepts of Chinese opera — it includes not only dialogue but also the essentials of traditional theatre, such as singing, movement and gesture, and martial arts. The emphasis is on theatricality, which constantly reminds the audience that they are not experiencing reality but watching a performance, and that they should thoroughly enjoy themselves in an exciting atmosphere not unlike that of a festival celebration (Gao 1984: 161–62). This is reminiscent of Bakhtin's idea of the carnival, but whereas Gao Xingjian's theatre can be considered in many ways "subversive," its main thrust is to recover drama's original *raison d'être*, to bring the theatre back to its very origin as a religious ritual, whereby people can enjoy spiritual and physical fulfilment, acquire happiness, or extricate themselves from suffering (Gao 1993: 191; Gao 1988a: 132). The idea of total theatre was carried over from *Wild Man* to *City of the Dead* (*Mingcheng* 冥城) (1987) and *Story of the Classic of Mountains and Seas* (*Shanhaijing zhuan* 山海經傳) (1989). These two plays, according to Gao Xingjian, sum up his pursuit of the idea of the theatre. They are not traditional Chinese opera, nor are they

Western opera; they feature music and dance, but they are not musicals in the general sense (Gao 1993: 190). With *City of the Dead*,

> [I] wish to break away from all the stylizations of traditional Chinese opera, including those of music, singing, dancing, and costuming, but preserve their various performing techniques, such as face-changing and acrobatics. … If someone were to ask me what I mean by "Modern Eastern Theatre," this play provides one of the answers." (Gao 1991: 243–44)

Contemporary theatre is characterized by the blurring of lines between different genres of performing art. The stage has become a melting pot, mixing drama with comedy routines, magic tricks, song and dance, and clowning techniques and devices. Meyerhold sees theatre as a "revue": when dancing, clowning, gymnastics, and acrobatics are incorporated into a play, they "can make the performance more diverting and deepen the spectator's comprehension of it." (Meyerhold 1998: 254) Artaud insists that "theatre's sphere is physical and plastic" (Artaud 2001: 137) and finds "spatial poetry" in the physicality of Balinese theatre and sign language (Artaud 2001: 104). In *The Theatre and Its Double* he writes:

> To link theatre with expressive form potential, with everything in the way of gestures, sound, colours, movement, is to return it to its original purpose, to restore it to a religious, metaphysical position, to reconcile it with the universe. (Artaud 2001: 136)

Both Meyerhold and Artaud's ideas have likely influenced Gao Xingjian's views on the theatre. To Gao, the ideal performance is a blend of physical action, dialogue, and psychology (Quah 2001: 164), but his theatre goes beyond Meyerhold's goal of deepening the audience's comprehension, even though that is also what Gao aims to achieve when he insists on communicating with the audience and providing them with a new perceptiveness. He is perhaps more at home with Artaud's idea of situating theatre at a metaphysical level. However, when Artaud proclaims that theatre exists "to express objectively secret truths, to bring out in active gestures those elements of truth hidden under forms in their encounters with Becoming" (Artaud 2001: 137), Gao would probably respond that his vision is more private, a "One Man's Bible," so to speak, or the insight one gets from understanding the self.

In 1988, Gao wrote an essay entitled "In Pursuit of a Modern Drama" (對一種現代劇的追求):

> Drama of the future is a kind of total drama. It is a kind of living drama with interactions between actors, actors and characters, characters, actors and audience being enhanced. It is different from the drama which is determined in the rehearsal room like canned products. It encourages spontaneous acting, which fills the theatre with vibrancy. It is like playing communal games. It fully develops every potential of the art. It will not be impoverished. It will collaborate with the artists of spoken language and avoid degenerating into mime or musical. It will be symphonized with multi-visuality. It will push the expressivity of language to its fullest capacity. It is an art that will not be substituted by another form of art. (Gao 1988b: 86, translated by Quah Sy Ren)

Thus his idea of the theatre is a living, vibrant theatre. It is interactive; it is like playing games in a communal setting; and it incorporates language and visual images which are expressive and multiple in its articulation. Furthermore, he aims not only for a multiform crossover, but also for an intercultural synthesis of Eastern and Western traditions. His total theatre aspires to combine the dialogic predilection of the West with the non-verbal physicality — gestures, movement and acrobatics — found in the theatre of the East, changing their techniques, breaking down the barrier between them and harmonizing their differences (Gao 1993: 186).

Eclecticism, then, is the key to Gao Xingjian's theatre. As he says of *Snow in August*:

> ... the story of Huineng is of epic proportions, on a par with any drama from the pen of Shakespeare. In fact, *Snow in August* melds Eastern and Western cultures. The form is like that of Shakespearian or Greek tragedy, but the spirit can only have come from the wisdom of the East. (Chang 2002a: 13)

With his characteristic avoidance of identification with the centre, he proceeds to "rewrite" on a peripheral platform the art forms belonging to the collective conscious (in this case Western opera and Beijing opera), that which he considers the main stream, according to his own design and preferences. Gao himself described his production of *Snow in August* as "four unlikes": unlike opera, unlike traditional Chinese drama, unlike dance, and unlike stage plays (Chang 2002c: 20). "It includes everything, but is not any one thing." It developed out of Beijing opera and Western opera but was neither, a new theatre that one day would make its way onto the world stage (Chang 2002a: 11).

With this in mind, what do we find in *Snow in August* that may help us better understand his idea of the theatre? The play is made up of three acts. The first two acts dramatize Huineng's life and death and portray the hero in bold strokes; more importantly, they make visible the spirit of Zen, of which he is the embodiment and manifestation. As the audience is led through the various episodes of Huineng's life, it appears that Gao Xingjian has abandoned the theatrical experiments of his previous plays and returned to a more traditional, language-based text. Meanwhile, Gao has also incorporated singing and comedic elements, which tend to loosen the plot. The play's structure is thus made to appear free and casual, breaking away from a naturalistic presentation of Huineng's life.

Unlike Acts I and II which feature a conventional plot structure, Act III is characterized by free form. It describes in a rather episodic manner, among other things, the practices of various schools of Zen Buddhism more than two hundred years after the death of Huineng. If it can be said to have a storyline — a fire in a Buddhist temple, it is not well defined. In fact, except for the similarity in setting and the presence of the Zen masters, the relevance to Huineng's story appears tenuous. Huineng passes away at the end of Act II, and for all practical purposes the story has ended when upon Huineng's death the trees and the mountains in the vicinity suddenly turn white — hence the title "Snow in August." So why Act III? What function does it serve? Gao has said that it is not necessary for a play to have a balanced or tightly knit plot, but despite having tried his hand at various dramatic forms, he still maintains that structural integrity is essential to any performance (Gao 1993: 187). A salient feature of Gao's plays in the 1990s is what I would call his "sideshows," which accompany and complement the main action. In *Between Life and Death* (1991), Woman's monologue is punctuated by non-speaking segments performed by Man (Woman's lover), a nun, a headless woman, and a man on stilts. In *Dialogue and Rebuttal* (1992), a monk is always present performing acrobatic tricks alongside the protagonists. These "sideshows" enrich the main action, sometimes providing commentary, sometimes serving as a stimulus for the audience to think and feel for themselves. In light of this, Act III of *Snow in August* is not so atypical, as it can be regarded as an expansion of the sideshow in many of Gao's plays — a sideshow writ large.

But then again, Act III is more than a sideshow: it is structurally and thematically more important. Hu Yao-heng proposes that Act III depicts an "atmosphere of desolation and absurdity," and that as the people and the Zen masters are shown to be "shallow" in their understanding of Zen, Act III is a reflection of the period of decline of the Buddhist school founded by Huineng (Hu 2002: 25–26). My view is that the play ends on a positive note. If we say that Huineng's story in the early part of the play expounds an understanding of Zen in abstract terms, then Act III is the actualisation of life as it should be lived, and if Acts I and II describe the spirit of a saintly patriarch, Act III is the embodiment of that spirit among the people in their everyday lives.

Act III, made up of a number of short episodic sketches, is a kaleidoscope of human activities. First we find Singsong Girl and Writer singing a duet, in which she invokes the names of famous Zen masters, all of whom are Huineng's disciples and their students. This signifies the passage of time — for instance, Caoshan Benji was the sixth generation disciple of Huineng — and that Zen Buddhism has spread far and wide in China in the span of 250 years. The names are also semantically significant, as they all point to Zen images and symbols. The song is followed by short sketches made up of *koan* questions : What is Buddha? Where is Buddha? The answers are implicitly provided by the ensuing scenes — Buddha is everywhere and resides in all things. Buddha can be found in moving and splitting bricks, carrying wooden planks, practicing martial arts, doing acrobatic tricks, performing "face changing," squabbling with one another, singing songs, and doing crazy things. This is reinforced by Singsong Girl's repetition of her song at the beginning of the Act, again invoking the names of Huineng's disciples, the Zen masters who have become Buddhas. Then there is the cat-chasing and fire-setting farce, with many characters running around on stage, culminating in Big Master "chopping" (presumably) the cat into two halves, which is one of the manifestations of "craziness" in the Zen Buddhist repertoire. The finale consists mainly of songs sung by all the on-stage characters: Singsong Girl, Writer, all the monks and laymen.

They sing of life and death, sickness and health, war and disaster, and the succession of the old by the new, in other words, all the conditions of being human. Life goes on as it should, and the best attitude is to carry on leading our lives as usual and doing the things we have to do. In this way, one will find Buddha and enlightenment. As Gao says, "Zen does not manufacture mystery; it is an understanding. It is eating, drinking, shitting, pissing, and sleeping as usual. It is only an attitude towards living, a thorough understanding of the world and of life." (Gao 1992c: 195) The idea is not to strive; with non-action and no-mind, one will achieve enlightenment living in the human world and doing worldly things.

Gao Xingjian always talks about the creative impulse in terms of an "inner pulsing":

> The making of an artist is due to his ability to relate his shadowy feelings and impulses to observable images. The "aesthetic sphere"(*yijing* 意境), so valued in Chinese art and poetry, is entrusting one's mental state to scenery and reaching the spirit by means of images." (Gao 2001b: 189–90)

The same principle informs *Snow in August*, i.e. the spirit of "big freedom" of Zen is revealed through the description of Huineng's life, the *indépendance totale* which allows him to act as he pleases to achieve Buddhahood.

To Gao Xingjian, freedom is of the utmost importance in life as in art. Thus the idea of complete abandonment and the latent anti-establishment inclination of Zen appeal to him tremendously. He values his freedom living in exile in France, and he talks about theatre and freedom in the same breath, hoping that the theatrical form, as performance, can enjoy the same kind of freedom as in fiction, poetry and other literary genres. In his view, the theatre is not free — it is bound by its inherent spatial and temporal limitations, the conventions of scene divisions and the "dead-end alley" of naturalism. In his pursuit of a new theatrical form, Gao strives for the kind of freedom that is not restricted by space or time, something akin to the freedom enjoyed by traditional Chinese opera and literature. When this is accomplished,

> all kinds of spatial and temporal relationships are possible in the theatre, interweaving fantasy and reality, recollections and imaginations, thinking and dreams, and symbols and narration. The result is multi-level visual imagery. And when this is accompanied by polyglossia, it will lead to

multiplicity, which is more appropriate for the molds of perception and thinking of modern men. (Gao 1988a: 137)

Gao's idea of "omnipotent theatre" is associated with and defined by his idea of freedom. As director of *Snow in August*, he wanted everything to start from zero. He required his actors, who had been schooled in Beijing opera, to "set aside [their] traditional moves and postures, set aside all the existing forms of Peking Opera, and start everything afresh" — they were to be spontaneous, and to extricate themselves from Beijing opera completely, so that they could develop the characters according to their own feelings towards their roles and the storyline (Chang 2002b: 13). *Snow in August* is the manifestation of Gao Xingjian's understanding of the essence of Zen (Fu 2002: 246), which has provided him with the inspiration and the means to carry out his ideas of theatre and dramatic performance. As he says, "Zen is both extrication and a spiritual sphere. Human beings are confined to a specific time and space, and they want to pursue freedom. Zen is an inspiration to artists living in the world of reality." (Gao 2001a: 146–47) In embodying an integrative vision of form and content, *Snow in August* comes close to being Gao Xingjian's ideal theatre.

A few words on the translation. My aim is to produce a close and faithful rendering of the play. I intend the translation to be natural, so that it will flow with the ease of original composition in English. However, there are also times when it is appropriate to preserve the Chineseness of the source text. The wordplays and puns are retained as much as possible, as are the songs and their rhymes — I try to resist the temptation to sacrifice sense and naturalness for the sake of rhyming.

The reader may find that the register of the dialogue may appear to fluctuate. At times it may appear formal, as befits the mannerisms, grace and solemnity of religious discourse; at other times it may be colloquial and closer to everyday conversation. This was done in adherence to the original style of the source text, which, like Gao Xingjian's theatre, seeks to be all-encompassing and integrative.

I hope that the translation can serve both as a performance text for the stage as well as a reading text, which can be enjoyed as literature and subjected to analysis with all the original literariness intact and unsullied.

Translation is always a matter of choice and balance. I also hope that I have made the right choices and struck the right balance that this fascinating theatrical piece deserves.

I wish to extend my thanks to Professor Peter Crisp of the English Department, Chinese University of Hong Kong for reading through the manuscript and making valuable suggestions, and to Ms. Jennifer Eagleton of the Translation Department of the Chinese University of Hong Kong, my daughter Natalia and my son Ian for their assistance in editing and proofreading.

Gilbert C. F. Fong

Note

1. Platform Sutra 壇經 (*Tan jing*), the influential Zen Buddhist classic, which has close to thirty different editions, was attributed to Huineng. It is also the only Buddhist sutra written by a Chinese master — Indian masters wrote all the others. The first few chapters of the book are Huineng's autobiography, which provide the sources for *Snow in August*. The ensuing chapters contain his lectures on Zen Buddhism. Fahai, Huineng's disciple, recorded the words of the master and compiled them into the book, to which he also wrote a preface. Even though *Snow in August* follows Huineng's story in the Platform Sutra quite closely, there are also a few minor changes. For example, the character Boundless Treasure is given more characterization and made more dramatic in the play. For a detailed analysis of the play's characters and their stories in historical records, please see Chen, 2002: 7–19.

References

Artaud, Antonin (2001). "The Theatre and Its Double," in *Artaud on Theatre,* ed. by Claude Schumacher with Brian Singleton. London: Methuen. Revised edition.

Chang Meng-jui 張夢瑞 (2002a). "Shashibiya ye fengkuang: Gao Xingjian tan *Bayue Xue* hua shiji yanchu" 莎士比亞也瘋狂：高行健談《八月雪》劃世紀演出 (An Epic Tale in the Making: An Interview with Gao Xingjian), trans. by Phil Newel. In *Ronghe dongxi, chaoyue chuantong. Bayue Xue pojian erchu*《融合東西，超越傳統：八月雪破繭而出》(A Groundbreaking Fusion of East and West, The Making of *Snow in August*). Taipei: Council for Cultural Affairs, pp. 10–24.

Chang Meng-jui 張夢瑞 (2002b). "Po jian er chu: *Bayue Xue* diaozhuo quanneng yanyuan" 破繭而出：八月雪雕琢全能演員 (Creating Holistic Performers for *Snow in August*), trans. by Robert Taylor. In *Ronghe dongxi, chaoyue chuantong. Bayue Xue pojian erchu*《融合東西，超越傳統：八月雪破繭而出》(A Groundbreaking Fusion of East and West, The Making of *Snow in August*). Taipei: Council for Cultural Affairs, pp. 12–17.

Chang Meng-jui 張夢瑞 (2002c). "Wu zhong sheng you you ruo wu: *Bayue Xue* yi quanxin xiju xingtai huan chanzong yuanmao" 無中生有有若無：《八月雪》以全新戲劇型態還禪宗原貌 (Made From Scratch: The Premiere of "Total Theater"), trans. by Phil Newel. In *Ronghe dongxi, chaoyue chuantong. Bayue Xue pojian erchu*《融合東西，超越傳統：八月雪破繭而出》(A Groundbreaking Fusion of East and West, The Making of *Snow in August*). Taipei: Council for Cultural Affairs, pp. 18–25.

Chen Hsiu-hui 陳秀慧 (2002). "*Bayue xue* ju zhong renwu de lishi fengmao"《八月雪》劇中人物的歷史風貌 (Historical records of the characters in *Snow in August*). *Performing Arts Journal*《台灣戲專學刊》, Dec. 2002, No. 5, pp. 7–19.

Fong, Gilbert C. F. (1999). "Introduction," in *The Other Shore: Plays by Gao Xingjian*, trans. by Gilbert C. F. Fong. Hong Kong: The Chinese University Press.

Fu Yu-hui 傅裕惠 (2002). "Zonglun *Bayue Xue* xin shiji xiqu yishu de linghang" 綜論《八月雪》，新世紀戲曲藝術的領航 (Some general comments on *Snow in August*: The helmsman of the art of drama and opera in the new century). *Performing Arts Journal*《台灣戲專學刊》, Dec. 2002, No. 5, pp. 232–46.

Gao Xingjian (1984). *Yeren* 野人 (Wild man). Taipei: Lianhe Wenxue, 2001.

Gao Xingjian (1988a). "Yao shenmeyang de xiju" 要什麼樣的戲劇 (What kind of drama do I want?). *Lianhe wenxue*《聯合文學》, No. 41.

Gao Xingjian (1988b). *Dui yizhong xiandaiju de zhuiqiu*《對一種現代劇的追求》(In pursuit of a modern drama). Beijing: Zhongguo Xiju Chubanshe (quoted in Quah, 1999: 94).

Gao Xingjian (1991). "Wode xiju he wode yaoshi" 我的戲劇和我的鑰匙 (My kind of drama and the key to my writing), in Gao Xingjian, *Meiyou zhuyi*《沒有主義》(None-ism). Hong Kong: Cosmos Books, 1996.

Gao Xingjian (1992a). "Zhongguo liuwang wenxue de kunjing" 中國流亡文學的困境 (The dilemma of Chinese exile literature), in Gao Xingjian, *Meiyou zhuyi*《沒有主義》(None-ism). Hong Kong: Cosmos Books, 1996.

Gao Xingjian (1992b). "Some Suggestions on Producing *Dialogue and Rebuttal*," in

The Other Shore: Plays by Gao Xingjian, trans. by Gilbert C. F. Fong. Hong Kong: The Chinese University Press, 1999.

Gao Xingjian (1992c). "'*Duihua yu fanjie' daobiaoyan tan*"《對話與反詰》導表演談 (On directing and acting in *Dialogue and Rebuttal*), in Gao Xingjian, *Meiyou zhuyi*《沒有主義》(None-ism). Hong Kong: Cosmos Books, 1996.

Gao Xingjian (1993). "Ling yizhong xiju" 另一種戲劇 (Another kind of drama), in Gao Xingjian, *Meiyou zhuyi*《沒有主義》(None-ism). Hong Kong: Cosmos Books, 1996.

Gao Xingjian (2001a). "Shijian, kongjian yu chan" 時間、空間與禪 (Time, space and Zen), in *Wenxue de liyou*《文學的理由》(The reason for literature). Hong Kong: Ming Pao Press.

Gao Xingjian (2001b). "Yijing yu zizai" 意境與自在 (Aesthetic sphere and being at ease), in *Wenxue de liyou*《文學的理由》(The reason for literature). Hong Kong: Ming Pao Press.

Gao Xingjian (2002). "Chuangzao chu yizhong jianli zai dongfang chuan-tong xiju gongdishang de xiandai yinyue gewuju — yizhong chang, nian, zuo, da de quanneng de xiju" 創造出一種建立在東方傳統戲劇功底上的現代音樂歌舞劇 —— 一種唱、念、做、打的全能的戲劇 (Creating a modern music and dance theatre built on Oriental tradition — An omnipotent theatre of singing, dialogue, movement, and martial arts). *Performing Arts Journal*《台灣戲專學刊》, Dec. 2002, No. 5, pp. 5–6.

Hu, John Y. H. (2002). "August Snow: An Appreciation," trans. by Daniel T. Hu, in *Bayue xue*《八月雪》(August Snow) (Program volume). Taipei: Council for Cultural Affairs, Executive Yuan, pp. 24–27.

Meyerhold, Vsevolod (1998). *Meyerhold on Theatre*, ed. and trans. by Edward Braun. London: Methuen. Revised edition.

Quah Sy Ren (1999). "The Theatre of Gao Xingjian: Experimentation Within the Chinese Context and Towards New Modes of Representation," Ph.D. dissertation. Faculty of Oriental Studies, The University of Cambridge.

Quah Sy Ren (2001). "Space and Suppositionality in Gao Xingjian's Theatre," in *Soul of Chaos: Critical Perspectives on Gao Xingjian*, edited by Kwok-kan Tam. Hong Kong: The Chinese University Press.

Zhao Yiheng 趙毅衡 (1999). *Jianli yizhong xiandai chan ju: Gao Xingjian yu Zhongguo xiandai shiyan xiju*《建立一種現代禪劇：高行健與中國現代實驗戲劇》(Establishing a modern Zen drama: Gao Xingjian and contemporary Chinese experimental drama). Taipei: Erya Chubanshe 爾雅出版社.

Act I, Scene 1. The young Huineng.

Act I, Scene 1. Boundless Treasure: "Boundless troubles occupy …"

* *August Snow*, presented by the Council for Cultural Affairs, Taiwan, December 19–22, 2002. Directed by Gao Xingjian.

Act I, Scene 2. The *Dharma* is passed on at East Mountain Temple.

Act II, Scene 1. The "Wind and Banner Controversy"

Act II, Scene 3. Huineng gives his first lesson.

Act II, Scene 3. Singsong Girl: "… is there snow in August?"

Act III. Pandemonium reigns in the Hall of Worship.

Act III. Fire in the temple.

Snow in August

Our play traverses 250 years of Chinese history from the middle of the seventh century (High Tang Dynasty) to the end of the ninth century (Late Tang Dynasty). The legend of Huineng, the sixth Patriarch of Zen Buddhism is told in drama and song.

Characters in order of appearance:
Huineng, the sixth Patriarch (633–713)
Boundless Treasure, a Buddhist nun
Hongren, the fifth Patriarch (602–675)
Shenxiu, a Zen master (c. 606–706)
Lu Zhen, a painter
Huiming, a Buddhist monk
Yinzong, a Zen Master (627–713)
(Young) Shenhui, an apprentice Buddhist monk
Writer
Singsong Girl
Fahai, a Zen master
Xue Jian, Court Messenger
Shenhui (c. 684–c. 758)
Crazy Monk
Old Woman
This Master, That Master, One Master, Another Master, Quite Master, Nice Master, Right Master, Wrong Master, Old Master, Big Master, Monks, Discipline Teachers, Novice Monk, Messenger, Soldiers, and Laymen A, B, C, D, E, F, G, H, I. There are more than 30 characters in total.

Act I Scene 1

In which Huineng Listens to the Sutra on a Rainy Night

[*Enter Huineng in front of the curtain. He sports a short Chinese jacket and a cloth waistband, in which is tucked an axe used for cutting firewood. He has on straw sandals but no stockings. He is holding a carrying pole with iron tips. Sound of wooden clappers.*]

Huineng   Greetings, members of the audience!

I am Huineng. My original surname is Lu. I was born in New Prefecture in the twelfth year of the Zhenguan period of the Tang Dynasty. My father came from Fanyang. He was an official, but he offended the court and had his office taken from him. After returning to civilian life, my parents became exiles in Canton, a place far away from civilization. My father died when I was young, and my mother, being a widow with a young son, decided to move the family to Nanhai. So here I am, trying to eke out a living by cutting and selling firewood.

[*The curtain rises. Sound of wooden fish and fast clappers. There is an altar at stage centre, lit by a single lamp. A single incense stick is burning; its smoke forms circles which hover in the air. The nun Boundless Treasure is dressed in a Buddhist kasaya robe, her head wrapped in a piece of plain blue cloth. She is sitting cross-legged on a futon in front of the altar, her head lowered, her back facing the audience. She is chanting*] *the sutra while beating the wooden fish. She is mumbling, so the words are indistinct.*

Huineng approaches. He stands motionlessly beside her and listens to her chanting.

Boundless (*She stops beating the wooden fish but does not turn to look at Huineng.*)

Who is it?

Huineng It's me. I'm here to deliver firewood.

Boundless Just put it in the kitchen.

Huineng I've stacked it there neatly for you already.

Boundless I am chanting the sutra. Come back early tomorrow morning for your money.

Huineng I don't take money from anyone serving Buddha.

Boundless Amitabha. The grace of Buddha!

(*She beats the wooden fish three times then stops suddenly.*)

Why aren't you leaving?

Huineng I want to listen to your chanting.

Boundless (*She stands up and turns to leave.*)

It's getting late. I have to close the doors now.

(*She looks up, revealing her bright eyes and delicate facial features. She is in her prime and obviously in possession of grace and beauty.*)

Huineng I'll go and close the doors for you. Just leave them to me.

Boundless If you want to listen to our chanting, you should come here early. We regularly hold our morning chanting sessions at four o'clock. You can join us if you want to.

Huineng I have to go up the mountain to cut firewood before the cock crows three times in the morning. I'm afraid I won't be able to come and listen to your chanting. Our family is very poor, and I have to support my aging mother. I really cannot come in the morning. I hope you will forgive me.

Boundless We followers of Buddha aim at delivering humanity from their miseries. There is no need to speak of forgiveness.

Huineng	Can I stay by your side and listen to your chanting, if it's not too much trouble?
Boundless	The temple has rules. I presume you are familiar with them. Even though I'm a nun, I'm still a woman and I should avoid being here with you. If you really wish to become a monk, you should take this copy of the sutra and recite the words of wisdom in it. Then you will have obtained some merit for yourself.
Huineng	I wouldn't know any words even if they were as big as a rice dipper. My family is poor, and I never went to school. If I had a copy of the sutra in my hand, I wouldn't be able to understand a single word.
Boundless	(*Thinks to herself.*)
	What should I do now? I'm a nun, and I should not get caught in any romantic entanglement. That was the reason I decided to seek refuge here at the Mountain Stream Temple! But now …
	Deep autumn, early chill, the raindrops hit the banana leaves. The night is long, and this young woodcutter insists on staying by my side. He refuses to leave the temple. What should I do? Amitabha, what should I do?
Huineng	It's fine with me. Please keep on chanting. I'll stay by your side and listen. Just ignore me.
Boundless	If you don't know any words, how can you understand what I am chanting just by listening? (*Beats the wooden fish twice then stops. Thinks to herself.*)
	Maybe this guy has an ulterior motive or something wicked on his mind?
Huineng	When we're thinking we don't need to write anything down. Especially with the profound wisdom of Buddha nature, how can it be explained by words? Why should literacy be a barrier? Please go on chanting. I'm listening. (*Boundless Treasure resumes her position, beats the wooden fish and starts to chant rapidly.*)
Huineng	You're chanting too fast.

	(*Boundless Treasure turns to look at Huineng and frowns.*)
Huineng	The words can't get into your heart if you chant so fast. (*Boundless Treasure beats the wooden fish and chants slowly.*)
Huineng	Now you're too slow. You see, the sentences are all cut up and the thoughts broken.
Boundless	Do you want to listen or not?
Huineng	(*Takes one step forward and leans to one side, paying full attention.*)
	I'm all ears.
Boundless	(*Thinks to herself.*)
	This guy is a real pain! (*Beats the wooden fish continuously.*) (*Music.*)
Huineng	(*Thinks to himself and turns to look at the nun.*)
	What's her problem? I thought nuns didn't have problems.
Boundless	(*Thinks to herself.*)
	A woodcutter, and he knows not a single word! How can I make him understand?
	(*Rubs her hands.*)
	Cut, cut, cut, let me cut out his delusions.
	(*She lowers her head to untie her blue head cloth and reveals her shaved head. Turning around, she finds herself face to face with Huineng. She starts to sing in a high-pitched voice.*)
	Boundless Treasure am I —
	Boundless troubles occupy.
Huineng	(*Sings.*)
	Hair can be cut and thrown away,
	But it's not as easy,
	To keep troubles at bay.
Boundless	(*Sings.*)
	From Spring to Autumn,
	Day after day,
	A lonely lamp is my only company
	To keep loneliness away.
Huineng	(*Sings.*)

	From sunrise to sunset,
	I cut and carry firewood.
	I'll cut more and more,
	And sell as much for my livelihood.
Boundless	(*Sings.*)
	Long and endless is the night,
	Who'll understand my plight?
Huineng	(*Sings.*)
	Year after year,
	What do I want for myself?
Boundless	(*Sings.*)
	Boundless Treasures am I,
	Boundless troubles occupy …
Huineng	(*Sings.*)
	I don't understand why …
Boundless	(*Sings.*)
	The night rain hits the banana leaves,
	The wind and the rain,
	When will they ever end?
Huineng	(*Sings.*)
	The thoughts keep coming,
	Now and then,
	Then and now.
	They can't be cut,
	They can't be blocked.
Boundless	(*Sings.*)
	Endless regrets,
	Boundless remorse;
	Endless and boundless sorrow.
Huineng	(*Sings.*)
	Is it true,
	Troubles lead to *Bodhi*?
	And Nirvana is the other shore?

[*The stage turns dark. Huineng steps forward as the curtain comes down behind him. One clap of the soundboard.*

Huineng   One day, Huineng went to a store after selling firewood in the market. There he saw a man reading the Diamond Sutra at the front. He stopped and listened and his mind was illuminated. He asked the man, "Sir, where did you find this sutra?" And the man answered, "I went to pay my respect to Hongren, the old master at the East Mountain Temple in Yellow Plum County and he presented the sutra to me. He has nearly a thousand disciples, including monks and laymen. And he enlightens the people with this sutra, which reveals the true nature of things, so that they may all become Buddhas on the instant."

[*Silence. Huineng focuses his thoughts and meditates. Exit.*

Act I Scene 2

In Which the *Dharma* Is Passed on at East Mountain Temple

[*Thuds of pounding rice.*
Enter Hongren. He stops and listens.
Enter Shenxiu hurriedly. He is good-looking and personable.

Hongren	(*Raises his hand.*) Instructor Shenxiu.
Shenxiu	Yes, Patriarch. (*Stands in attention at once. Clasps his hands in greeting.*) What is your wish?
Hongren	Who is pounding rice down the hall?
Shenxiu	A young layman. His surname is Lu, and he is known as Huineng. I'm not sure if that's his ordination name. As far as I know he has not been ordained. He's been here for about eight months now. When he first arrived I brought him here to have an audience with Your Holiness.
Hongren	Yes, I remember him now. He's the barbarian from the south. As soon as he opened his mouth, he said he wanted nothing but to become a Buddha.
Shenxiu	What arrogance! An out and out savage from the mountains. And he even dared to talk back to Your Holiness.
Hongren	(*Smiles.*) He talks as he thinks. Don't mind him. It's not his fault. Don't hold a grudge against him.
Shenxiu	At least he's honest. Every day he pounds rice in the shed and talks very little.
Hongren	His words are few but every word is to the point. Do you remember what he told me? He said, "You can

separate men into northerners and southerners, but you can't divide Buddha nature into north and south. Barbarians are not monks, but what difference is there in their Buddha nature?"

Shenxiu   Who does he think he is? This is really preposterous.

Hongren   Someone that discerning can't be all that bad. If that was really his idea, then he's not doing too badly. Today I'm going to give a lecture on the Supreme Sutra. Inform all the monks and staff to drop whatever they're doing when they hear the bell, and come immediately to the assembly hall. Invite the monks and laymen who are staying with us at the temple as well. I have something to tell everybody.

Shenxiu   Yes, master. Should I also invite Lu the painter to come? We've commissioned him to paint two pictures: "The Transfiguration of the Assembly in the Lankavatara Sutra" and "The Buddha Passes on His Robe."

Hongren   This doesn't concern him. Let him think in peace. Have the walls in the hallway been whitewashed?

Shenxiu   Please be reassured. Everything has been kept neat and tidy, ready for the painter to do his job tomorrow.

Hongren   In that case, leave me.

[*Exit Shenxiu. Hongren listens to the sound of pounding rice. The bell tolls loudly and the pounding stops. Enter the monks one by one. Hongren ascends the hall. The tolling stops.*

Hongren   (*Goes up the pulpit.*)
                 All disciples and followers, let your hearts be at peace. (*All clasp their hands and lower their heads.*)

Hongren   I don't have much to say to you. I've said all I wanted to say already in past lectures. At any rate, all that which can be spoken is not the real meaning of the *Dharma*. It is something you have to comprehend for yourself. Day and night you people are busy worshipping and paying homage to Buddha, trying only to cultivate the

field of merits, but you never ask yourself the big
question of life and death. If you can't extract yourself
from the bitter sea of life and death, what is it that you
aspire to? If you have lost your self-nature, what is the
use of the field of merits? Do you think you will be able
to save yourself from suffering in this way?
What are you staring at? There is no use staring at me.
Go and stare at yourselves! Return to your rooms. If you
possess wisdom, you should let yourself be enlightened
of your own *prajna*, your innate wisdom.
(*The crowd look at one another, not knowing what to do.*)

Hongren   Have you not come to my temple to seek Buddha? Now
go and compose a *gatha* poem and show it to me. If any
one of you can prove that he has understood the truth of
Buddha in his *gatha*, then I will pass on the *Dharma* to
him, and he will inherit the robe and the almsbowl,
which have been handed down for five generations since
the Bodhidharma, and become the Sixth Patriarch.

[*Exit Hongren. Crowd scurry around in confusion, not
knowing what to do.*
Shenxiu, bewildered, stands on one side, his head lowered.

Crowd   Look, come and take a look!
What the hell are you looking at? You're stepping on my
shoes!
Instructor Shenxiu, he must have got it already.
They didn't make him the principal instructor for
nothing. Don't waste your time.
Don't worry, after Instructor Shenxiu receives the
Dharma, we'll just follow him and chant our sutra. We'll
be all right.
(*Huiming, martial arts instructor, walks through the hall,
strutting and swaggering.*)

Crowd   Instructor Huiming!
Have you got it?

	(*Huiming ignores them. Exit.*)
Crowd	You think he's got it already?
	Him? If you asked him to fight, he wouldn't have a problem for sure. But writing? That's a different story!
	(*Exit Crowd.*)
Shenxiu	(*Paces back and forth, rubs his palms continuously, and talks to himself.*)

The Patriarch has a thousand disciples, but no one dares to write this *gatha*.

As principal instructor, I'll have to write it even if nobody will. I'm the only one to do it.

If I were to plot, if I were to take over the Patriarchate for myself.... Even the thought of it is not right. I can't possibly force myself to do that, not under any circumstances.

(*Ruminates.*)

If I don't present this *gatha* to the Patriarch, then he won't be able to know how deeply I have understood the sutra, and I won't be able to become the true successor and inherit the *Dharma*. What am I to do? What am I to do! (*Exit.*)

[*Silence. The stage turns dark. The nightwatchman's drum starts thumping.*
Enter Shenxiu holding a candle. He is very watchful and looks here and there.

Shenxiu The watchman has struck for the second watch. All the rooms are silent. When I first became a monk, I only wanted to serve the Patriarch and to purify my mind, so that it would be free from doubt. I have never been ambitious; I have never thought about succeeding the Patriarch. Now the old master wants to pass on the robe and the almsbowl, but his intention is unclear. What is to be done?

(*Listens to the drum.*)

Luckily no one knows what I'm doing here!
(*He takes out a brush from inside his sleeve, removes the cap and writes in a frenzy on the wall, reciting.*)
The body is a *Bodhi* tree,
The mind a mirror bright,
Always wipe it clean,
And let no dust alight. (*Exit.*)

[*The bells ring for the morning chanting session. One by one the monks hurry across the stage, which gradually lights up. Enter Lu Zhen the painter carrying an ink slab and a brush. He swaggers forward, swaying left and right as he walks. Percussion music.*

Lu   I'm Wonder Brush Lu Zhen!
As a painter, I have painted everything under the sun, all of them in beautiful colors and vivid detail. From the gods in Heaven to the ghosts and demons in hell, and from the Queen Mother of the West to Cow Head and Horse Face, the guards at the entrance to Hades, not to mention kings, generals and ministers, boudoirs and studies, and even the secrets of inner chambers. There is but one picture I still haven't painted, the portrait of Master Bodhidharma from Western Heaven. I don't know if he had long ears drooping down to his shoulders, or if he had horns growing on his forehead. Lucky for me no one has seen him in person either.
(*Suddenly looks up.*)
What's going on here? Yesterday this was a nice, clean white wall, but some scoundrel has scribbled graffiti on it. How impudent and disrespectful! This is no ordinary drafting paper. It's to be the sacred spot, a place of worship, after a portrait of Bodhidharma has been painted on it. Now it's been defiled and totally ruined! Outrageous indeed! ... Anybody here?
(*Enter a Novice Monk hurriedly.*)

Novice	Master Lu, what's happened to you? Have you hurt your foot or something?
Lu	Your master has not hurt his foot, thank you very much. Take a look at this wall! Who did this? Do you recognize the writing? The impudent rascal!
Novice	I haven't got a clue. The words are all messed up.
	(*Enter an Old Monk. He takes a look at the wall.*)
Old Monk	Amitabha! Go and tell the Patriarch at once!

[*Exit Novice running. Enter Crowd. They gather in front of the wall trying to identify the handwriting.*
Enter Hongren.

Hongren	(*Ponders for a moment.*)
	All physical forms, all phenomena and images are but illusions. Master Lu, you don't have to paint the portrait any more. Since you have traveled a long way to come here, please accept my gift of three silver ingots for your troubles. Leave the *gatha* on the wall. All of you may study it and cultivate your virtues accordingly. In this way you will not fall and suffer from the evil realms of existence. Well done! Well done!

[*Crowd reads and recites the* gatha. *Lu thanks Hongren and exits.*
Enter Shenxiu. He stands motionlessly, his head lowered. Upon seeing him, Crowd clasp their hands in greeting then exit.

Hongren	Did you write this *gatha*?
Shenxiu	(*Steps forward and bows.*)
	Please forgive the mistake your disciple has committed. I know that it is improper of me to seek the patriarchate. My only hope is for Your Holiness to bestow on me great mercy and pity, and to judge how much wisdom there is in me, and whether I have acquired a general under- standing of the *Dharma*.

Hongren	You haven't entered the room. You have just reached the door.
Shenxiu	Your humble disciple lacks intelligence. He awaits the master's elucidation.
Hongren	At ease. If you want to obtain the ultimate enlightenment, you have to look for it in your self-nature.
Shenxiu	How does one look for self-nature? Your humble disciple does not understand.
Hongren	Strive to purify your mind, then write another *gatha* and let me see it! If you show that you are capable of entering the room through the door, then I will pass the robe and the *Dharma* truth onto you. (*Exit.*)

[*Shenxiu watches the back of Hongren as he exits. Exit Shenxiu.*
Sound of pounding rice. At the back of the stage, Huineng is treading on the wooden lever of the rice-pounding machine, his feet going up and down. A big stone is tied to his waist. Enter Novice Monk.

Novice	(*Recites as if singing.*) The body is a *Bodhi* tree, The mind a mirror bright …
Huineng	(*Stops treading.*) Novice, what are you singing?
Novice	The Patriarch told us to sing the *gatha* Instructor Shenxiu had written on the wall in the great hall. He also told us to study it. (*Exit.*)

[*Faint chanting is heard off stage. Lento: "Always wipe it clean, And let no dust alight …"*
Huineng unties the stone on his waist and looks for where the chanting is coming from. Exit.
Chanting stops.
Sound of wooden fish. Allegretto. Enter Lu Zhen carrying his painting supplies. He is walking hurriedly.

Enter Huineng from the other side.)

Huineng	Mr. Painter …
Lu	(*Surprised.*) Oh!
Huineng	What kind of sutra is written on this wall?
Lu	The characters are like black earthworms. They're just a scrawl, totally devoid of energy or discipline. Nothing worth mentioning!
Huineng	May I trouble Mr. Painter to write a few words for this unworthy servant?
Lu	Do you prefer vermilion or emerald?
Huineng	The wall is white, so I guess black will do. As long as people can read the words clearly.
Lu	There are five shades of black, which can also be dark or light, or glossy or matte.
Huineng	Please do as you see fit.
Lu	Do you want me to write in seal script, official script, running script, cursive script, or regular script?
Huineng	Anything is fine as long as the words are neat and tidy.
Lu	Then speak slowly. Master Painter Lu Zhen at your service. (*Tucks in his sleeve and takes out his ink and brush.*)
Huineng	The *Bodhi* is not a tree,
	Nor the mind a mirror bright;
	Buddha nature is always pure,
	Where can any dust alight?
Lu	(*Wields his brush and writes quickly.*)
	There, there, now it's done.
	(*Exit Huineng quietly.*)
Lu	(*Looks left and right in admiration.*)
	What insight! Excellent! What a wonderful *gatha*!

[*Lu turns and finds Huineng gone, puts away his painting supplies into a knapsack, which he carries on his back, and exits. Sound of rice pounding. The stage turns dark. Huineng is seen treading on the lever of the rice-pounding machine. The wind starts to blow.*

*Enter Hongren carrying a lantern, hobbling along. He raises
the lantern to read the writing on the wall, and then he blows
out the light.*
*The wind blows hard. Huineng stops working and unties the
stone at his waist.*

Huiming	(*Looks into the dark.*) Who is it?
Hongren	It's me, your Patriarch.
Huineng	Has the master not retired yet?
Hongren	There's something on my mind that I can't let go.
Huineng	Can it ever be let go?
Hongren	(*Hits mortar thrice with the lantern rod.*)
	The rice, have you finished pounding it yet?
	(*Huineng fills a bamboo dipper with rice, raises the dipper and pours the rice out into a bamboo basket, which makes a sizzling sound.*)
Hongren	(*Arches his back to whisper into Huineng's ear.*)
	Come to my chamber. I'll elucidate the *Dharma* to you.
	(*Exits into the dark.*)

[*Huineng straightens himself and listens. The wind howls then
stops, and then all becomes quiet.*
*On one side of the stage, Huiming, his eyes lowered, is seen
standing on a stump in front of the drum stand. He is standing
on one leg and his hand is holding an incense stick that has
almost burnt out. He dozes off, his body sways and he tips and
falls from the stump. It is a sudden awakening. He picks up a
drumstick by the stand and beats the drum thrice.*

Huineng	Huiming, Huiming, you have failed to live up to your fame.
	(*Shakes his head continuously.*)
	You're tall and handsome, and you're a general of the third rank. But all is in vain.
	You really wanted to understand the *Dharma*, so you came running here to study with the old Patriarch. You

study every day and night, and you've been cultivating
your virtues year after year, but you still lose out in the
end. (*Exit.*)

[*At centre stage, Hongren is holding a candlestick in front of
his meditation bed, his back facing the audience.
Enter Huineng. He stands outside the door.*

Hongren	Who is it outside the door?
Huineng	It's Huineng, the layman.
Hongren	What are you doing standing outside?
Huineng	I'm still hesitating, wondering if I'm good enough, good enough to enter through the door.
Hongren	Just take one step forward and you're in.
Huineng	(*Takes three steps forward and bows.*)
	Your humble servant awaits the instruction of the Patriarch!
Hongren	You've come from the outside, what do you see outside the door?
Huineng	A world of myriad phenomena, the sun, the moon, mountains and rivers, wandering clouds and flowing water, and unending wind and rain.
	In this world there are dogs, horses, sedan chairs, carriages, and high officials and their lackeys. They keep coming and going.
	And then there are merchants and tradesmen, shouting at the top of their voices and striving to hawk their wares; people who are suffering and who have to swallow their bitterness; and men and women infatuated with love, their lives turned upside down.
	It's now late at night, all is quiet, only the cries of a newborn baby are heard.
Hongren	What do you see inside the door?
Huineng	The Master and I.
Hongren	(*Laughs.*)
	What am I?

Devant et derrière la porte 門之內外 Gao Xingjian 124.5 × 87.5 cm 1996

Huineng	A *ksana*, a thought in the mind.
Hongren	Where is it?
Huineng	From one thought to another, it is everywhere.
Hongren	(*Hollers.*)
	No, it's nowhere, nowhere to be found. So what is there to think about?
Huineng	(*Silent, his head lowered. Raises his head after a short moment.*)
	Nothing.
Hongren	Why did you say there was?
Huineng	Only because the Master asked just now…
Hongren	There is no just now!

[*A heavy drumbeat is heard coming from the dark. Hongren turns and picks up a wooden staff from beside his bed. He turns back and draws a circle on the floor.*

Huineng	(*Bends down to look at the circle, then looks up.*)
	It's empty.

[*Another heavy drumbeat. Hongren raises the staff and draws another circle.*
Huineng raises his head and looks at Hongren with a smile.
One more heavy drumbeat.

Hongren	(*Laughs: Ha! Ha!*)
	This shows that you are cognizant of your self-nature, a zealous disciple, a teacher of Heaven and men, a Buddha! This is great wisdom leading to the other shore!

[*Fourth heavy drumbeat.*
Hongren returns to his bed, sits up straight, and holds the robe and almsbowl in both hands.

Hongren	This is the robe Master Bodhidharma wore when he traveled east from India to China. He passed the robe

on to the Second Patriarch Huike, Huike passed it on to Sengcan, Sengcan passed it on to Daoxin, Daoxin passed it on to me, Hongren, and now I'm passing it on to you. I now pronounce you the Sixth Patriarch.

This is the bowl I carried with me when I traveled to beg for alms. I'm leaving it to you as well. Guard your thoughts well and deliver all the unenlightened from their sufferings.

Huineng The *Dharma* is transmitted from mind to mind. What then is the use of this robe?

Hongren The robe is proof of the *Dharma*, which is the genesis of the robe. It has been passed on from generation to generation, so that the lamp of the mind will not be extinguished.

Huiming (*Receives the robe and the almsbowl with both hands and bows.*)

My heart-felt gratitude to the Master!

Hongren It has always been like this: He who receives the *Dharma* will have his life hanging by a thread. If you stay here, I'm afraid someone may harm you. You must leave at once!

Huiming Where should I go? I hope the Master can show me the way.

Hongren The spring of wisdom in this temple has run dry. Take a look at this mammoth temple. It boasts a large number of temple-goers and visitors, who all insist that they are here in search of Buddha, but every one of them is motivated by greed, hungry for instant fame and fortune. I really don't understand why they have come. Central China is a land of many disputes, where Buddha's Law will not be allowed to prosper, and heresies will rise and compete with one another. The heretics will ingratiate themselves with the rich and the powerful and pander shamelessly to the imperial court. You came from south of the mountains, so you should go back there and live in seclusion. After that you should devote yourself to

	enlightening the deluded beings and delivering them from their ignorance.
Huiming	How about Master yourself?
Hongren	I have fulfilled my destiny. After you are gone, I shall say my farewell to this world.
	(*Fifth heavy drumbeat.*)
Hongren	Follow me, I'll open the temple door for you!

[*Hongren leads Huineng. Exit both into the dark.*
Five drumbeats indicating the fifth watch, followed by loud
and continuous tolling of the bell. Enter Huiming.

Huiming	(*Rubs his eyes and shakes his head.*)
	I bolted the door myself last night. I remember it clearly. It's now the fifth watch and the dawn still hasn't broken but the door is already wide open!
	(*Picks up the door bolt on the ground.*)
	The monks have just heard the bell and gotten out of bed. They still haven't started their morning chanting yet. Some burglars must have sneaked in here and stolen the temple treasures.
	Burglars! Burglars! Come and catch the burglars! Don't let them get away!

[*Enter Hongren leisurely. Also enter Crowd, scurrying in*
confusion.

Hongren	The house of Buddha is quiet and peaceful, why are you hollering and making so much noise?
Huiming	The temple door is wide open. We've been burglarized!
Hongren	The house of Buddha is empty, what do we have here that's worth stealing? I opened the door myself. The Great *Dharma* has been pronounced. Go purify your heart and cultivate your own virtues.
Huiming	Master, to whom have you passed on the Great *Dharma*?
Hongren	A layman from New Prefecture.

Huiming	That southern barbarian in the rice-pounding shop? Why do you still ask me to do the meaningless good works then? The Great *Dharma* has been stolen already.
Hongren	If that's what you think, go away. Go away, all of you.
Huiming	Go at once to catch the *Dharma* thief! (*Exit running, carrying the door bolt in his hand.*)
	(*Exit all except Hongren hurriedly.*)
Hongren	Evil beings! They'll never understand …

[*Enter Shenxiu in travelling garb.*

Shenxiu	Your humble student is ashamed of himself!
Hongren	Where are you going?
Shenxiu	I'm going to travel around central China to acquire more knowledge. I aim to improve myself.
	(*Kowtows.*)
	Master, please take care of yourself. (*Exit.*)
Hongren	(*Looks up at the sky.*)
	It's time for me to bid farewell to the human world. (*Exit.*)

Act I Scene 3

In Which Huineng Runs Away
from Disaster

[Enter Huineng. He is carrying a cloth knapsack on his back.
His hands are performing a rowing movement.

Huineng   (*Sings.*)
The water flows and flows,
A strong wind drives the waves,
Set adrift is a lonely boat,
The Yangtze River it braves.
The *Dharma* is mine to keep,
I still have to run and hide,
Even Buddha finds the world
A trying place to reside.
(*Enter Huiming leading Crowd.*)

Huiming   Look! There's the boat!
The lowly stinking little brat, that's the guy!
Don't let him get away, go catch him at once!
He's got the old Buddha's robe and almsbowl. Tell him
to give them up. Leave them for us!
What are you looking at? Go and get the boat.

Crowd   (*Singing as they run.*)
Make haste, make haste,
Don't let him land before!
Or we'll be looking in vain
For the other shore, oh, the other shore!

Huineng   (*Sings.*)

It's all the same,

The human world or the western sky,

It's hard being a man,

Even harder a Buddha, if you try.

(*Huineng takes off his shoes, jumps off the boat and exits running.*)

Crowd (*Sing.*)

Great Wisdom, on the other shore,

Only fools give chase and dash out the door,

It's only futile,

Futile …

[*Enter Huineng barefooted, carrying a cloth knapsack on his back and holding his shoes in his hand.*

Huineng (*Sings.*)

Cross every river,

Climb every mountain.

Crowd (*Sing.*)

Search for the eternal and true,

It's tough going,

A tough going task to do!

Huineng (*Sings.*)

The temple shuts its door,

A wild man in the wilderness. (*Throws away his shoes and exits running.*)

Crowd (*Running and singing.*)

Better to fame and fortune find,

Easy on the body,

Easy on the mind. (*Exit.*)

[*Enter Huineng, holding an almsbowl and a staff. He throws down the knapsack, panting.*

Huineng (*Sings.*)

Mount Dayi is bare and drear,

The wind howling,
The spring water cold and clear.
Huineng, where can you rest your life?
The *Dharma* is with dangers rife.

[*Murmuring sound of running water. Huineng opens the knapsack, takes out the almsbowl and stoops to ladle water with it.*
Enter Huiming hurriedly with a wooden club.

Huiming	(*Hollers.*) You son of a bitch! I've been looking for you for a long, long time. Let me give you a piece of my club! (*Huiming tries to club Huineng, who turns a somersault and dodges the blow, still holding the almsbowl in his hand.*)
Huiming	Give me your life or the robe and almsbowl!
Huineng	(*Extends his hand, which is holding the almsbowl.*) Here, take it … (*Huiming makes a swipe and threatens to strike Huineng, then leaps across, trying to snatch the almsbowl.*)
Huineng	Take this and go begging with it! (*Lets go of the almsbowl, which shatters into pieces on the ground.*)
Huiming	(*Shocked, and then becomes furious.*) You rascal, you've broken the Patriarch's almsbowl into pieces! (*Raises his club.*) Your life or mine! Give me the Patriarch's robe!
Huineng	If you want it, it's yours.

[*Huineng leisurely opens the knapsack and takes out a robe. Huiming puts down the club and raises his hand, but he starts shaking continuously.*

Huineng	Master Huiming, the *Dharma* has no form!
Huiming	(*Kneels down instantly.*) Please forgive the mistake of this uncouth kung fu man! (*Kowtows.*) Please also forgive my ignorance, which led to my

	endless pursuit of you. My quest is only for the *Dharma*, not the robe. Please teach me and let me be enlightened!
Huineng	There's no need to stand on ceremony. Since you've come for the *Dharma*, let your heart be at peace and listen to my words.
	If you didn't contemplate goodness, and you didn't contemplate evil, then how could the true face of Master Huiming be seen?
	(*Huiming is speechless. He and Huineng look at each other. Huiming looks down.*)
Huineng	Go north and deliver people from their sufferings. (*Exit.*)

[*Huiming clasps his hands in salutation.*
Enter Crowd, looking anxious and frustrated.

Crowd	Master Huiming, have you seen the barbarian from the south?
Huiming	Have I seen that guy? No way! The wind has been blowing a gale on this big mountain ridge. Not a soul anywhere. The guy is lame in one foot. He's probably fallen into a hole somewhere. Maybe he's been eaten by a tiger or something. There isn't a single trace of him. Forget it! Go away! Go away! Go home and carry on with your lives! (*Exit.*)

[*Crowd disbands reluctantly. Exit.*

Act II Scene 1

In Which the "Wind and Banner Controversy" Occurs

[*Two monks are hoisting a banner in front of a huge incense burner below the steps leading to the central hall of a temple. On the banner it is written: "Neither Creation Nor Extinction." The name "Dharma Nature Temple" is inscribed on the bottom to one side.*

Monk A	"Neither Creation Nor Extinction." What does that mean?
Monk B	Mind your own business. They only told us to hoist the banner.
Monk A	Just try explaining it, okay? What does it mean?
Monk B	*Dharma* Master Yinzong is going to give a lecture on the sutra a little bit later, why don't you ask him then?
Monk A	You and I have come here to the Dharma Nature Temple for many years now. We've eaten our share of salt and chanted our share of sutras. But if the master asks us what kind of banner we've put up and we don't know how to answer him, then wouldn't all our efforts be a total waste?
Monk B	Hoisting a banner is also good works.
Monk A	This only applies to people with small natural capacity.
Monk B	And you've got big natural capacity?
Monk A	If we don't get to the bottom of things for the correct answers, how can we develop our capacity?
Monk B	Don't waste your time talking. Let's hurry and get this over with! You pull on that side and I'll unroll from this side.

[*The banner is hoisted and the two monks look up. The banner waves in the wind, and it waves more and more rigorously. Enter the monks one after another.*]

Monk C	It's so windy. Where did this wind come from?
Monk D	Make sure the banner doesn't fall and hit someone on the head. Did you tie a dead knot there?
Monk A	The knot is dead, but the head is alive.
Monk B	Never mind. Let it wave all it wants. Our job is done.

[*Enter Huineng. He is now middle-aged, wearing straw sandals and dressed in layman's clothing made of hemp. He looks at the banner.*
Silence. The banner is waving even more vigorously in the wind, making a flapping sound.]

Monk C	It's such a big banner, it must be really heavy as well. How come it keeps on flapping and fluttering?
Monk D	Because the wind sets the banner in motion. That's my explanation.
Monk C	But the wind is insentient, how come it moves the banner for no reason? Huh, try explaining that!
Monk E	The wind is invisible. It's the banner that moves.
Monk C	The banner is insentient as well. How come it moves by itself?
Monk F	It's true neither the wind nor the banner is sentient. They move because they are compatible in their respective *karma*.
Monk C	*Karma* belongs to the realm of sentient beings, therefore it is capable of movement. But the banner and the wind are both insentient, why do they also move?

[*Enter Master Yinzong.*

Yinzong	Good question! Who can answer it?
Monk D	When there is movement the wind is present, and when

	there is no movement the wind is absent. This is inherent in the wind's nature. The banner looks as if it's moving, but it's actually the wind moving by itself. It is a mistake to see only the banner moving and not the wind moving by itself.

Monk E   I beg to differ. A banner is capable of movement but a boulder isn't. When the wind blows, a banner moves but a boulder remains stationary. It is not in the nature of the wind but that of the banner to move, thus it is the banner moving itself with the wind.

Huineng   Both the wind and the banner are insentient, why then should you talk about their nature of motion or motion-lessness? The wind and the banner are themselves as thus. The banner does not move, nor does the wind. The movement we see is but an illusion in our mind. The *Dharma* originally makes no distinction between motion and motionlessness. This is the true meaning of "Neither creation nor extinction"!

Yinzong   Who is it that speaks?

Huineng   A layman passing by.

Yinzong   Please come forward and present yourself! May I ask what is your name?

Huineng   My surname is Lu. I'm known as Huineng.

Yinzong   Where did you come from?

Huineng   The mountains in the south.

Yinzong   Do you have a teacher?

Huineng   I was once under the tutelage of the Old Master Hongren in North Ridge, in a place called East Mountain in Qizhou.

Yinzong   You are aware that the Old Master has departed this earth?

Huineng   Yes, I've failed to live up to his faith in me.

Yinzong   I will not give a lecture on the sutra today. You all go back to your work. I have to converse with this lay brother.

(*Exit monks.*)

Yinzong	(*Whispering.*)
	Before Master Hongren died, he said that the *Dharma* would travel south. You must be the good person who holds the truth of the *Dharma*.
Huineng	Yes, I'm the one.
Yinzong	You have not begun to spread the words of the *Dharma*. Is there any reason for such tardiness?
Huineng	It was the Master's commandment that I should conceal myself for some time before revealing my identity. Therefore I've been hiding among a party of hunters in the counties of Sihui and Huaiji in Canton Prefecture.
Yinzong	Are you really the Fifth Patriarch's designated successor Huineng? Where are your credentials?
Huineng	I still have the Patriarch's robe in my possession.
Yinzong	Supreme *karma*! (*Clasps his hands in salutation.*)
	I was also once a disciple of Master Hongren and received instructions from him, but I was unable to apprehend the *Dharma* for my lack of intelligence. The few words you've just spoken overwhelmed me. Such wisdom I have never heard all my life. In comparison, my expositions on the Maha Parinirvana Sutra are like worthless dregs. Master, please allow me to lead you into the chamber!

[*Exit both.*

Act II Scene 2

In Which Huineng Receives the Commandments

[*Bell ringing. Enter Boundless Treasure ringing a Buddhist bell. She sports a tattered robe made of rags. Her head is shaved and her feet are bare. She is holding an almsbowl in her hand.*

Boundless   (*Loudly.*)
I'm a Buddhist nun. Boundless Treasure is my name!
Boundless treasure, boundless wonders, boundless profundity, and bound to be misunderstood!
(*Smiles. Rings the bell.*)

[*Enter Yinzong on the other side, leading a group of monks.*

Yinzong   (*Loudly.*)
Monks of all houses, instructors, and discipline teachers, let us welcome to the pulpit Master Huineng, true heir to the *Dharma* of the Fifth Patriarch Hongren!

Boundless   (*Walks across front stage, singing.*)
Boundless thoughts, boundless entanglements,
Boundless grievances, inextricable *karma*s,
Boundless pains and the boundless sea of bitterness —

[*Enter Huineng in Dharma robe, his hands clasped. The monks all clasp their hands in salutation.*

Yinzong   Now we will ask the three discipline teachers to come forward and take part in the incense burning ceremony. They are His Holiness Zhiguang, abbot of Zongchi Temple in Xijing, Master Huijing, head monk of the Lingguang Temple in Suzhou, and Master Daoying, instructor of the Tianhuang Temple in Jingzhou.

[*The three discipline teachers light the incense sticks.*

Boundless   (*Sings.*)
Boundless desires, boundless illusions,
Boundless prayers, and boundless asceticism.

[*The monks surround Huineng and inspect his robe. They are overawed and begin to talk among themselves.*

Monks   It's the real thing!
I've never seen anything like it!
What is it made of?
Is it made of real silk?
Huineng   It's made of cotton.
Monks   Really? My goodness!

[*Boundless Treasure rings the Dharma bell and begins to dance.*

Boundless   (*Sings loudly.*)
From Spring to Summer, Autumn and Winter,
To the east, the west, the north and the south,
From the edge of the sea to the edge of the earth,
A big void, with no border, no end in sight … (*Exit.*)

[*Yinzong ascends the pulpit.*

Yinzong   The tripitaka master Gunavarman of the Song Dynasty constructed this pulpit. At the time it was recorded that an *arhat* would ascend this pulpit, and a Bodhisattva would receive the commandments here. At this moment,

I, Abbot Yinzong of the Dharma Nature Temple, will perform the haircutting and shaving ceremony for Master Huineng. Discipline teachers, please bear witness to this service, as Master Huineng will receive the entire commandments and be fully ordained.

[*Bells toll simultaneously. Yinzong leads the way for Huineng and the three discipline teachers. They walk across the hall and exit.*
Sound of wooden fish. Monks chanting.

Monks (*Chanting together.*)
Good men and believing women,
Bodhisattvas and Mahasattvas,
Let this be so,
Control and humble the heart!
(*Exit in a line.*)

[*Enter Boundless Treasure, dancing with the Dharma bell in her hand.*

Boundless (*Loudly.*)
Troubles, troubles,
So many troubles,
This world of men!

[*Enter Crowd, following her.*

Crowd Look, come and take a look!
A mad woman!
Where? Where?
My goodness, a Buddhist nun!
Even the nun's going mad!

Boundless It's you who are mad. You pig heads, you refuse to be enlightened!

Crowd Sing! Sing again!

	Give her two coppers!
	Have pity on her!
Boundless	Have pity on you, all of you!
Crowd	Get out of the way, you idiot!
	Let people pass! You devil you!
	My goodness, she's got scabies all over her!
Boundless	Oh no, I don't. It's you who've got muck all over your bodies, not me!
Crowd	Leave her alone. She practices the *Dhuta* discipline. She wants to get rid of life's trials!
	An ascetic nun! Amitabha!
Boundless	(*Sings loudly.*)
	Oh Boundless Treasure, there is boundless treasure in you,
	Boundless wonders and boundless profundity ... (*Exit*)

[*Bell ringing fades.*

Act II Scene 3

In Which Huineng Gives His First Lesson
in the Pulpit

[*Pitter Patter of rain gradually becomes louder. Enter Huineng slowly. His head is shaved. He is dressed in a short gown made of coarse cloth and trousers, the legs of which are tied. He also has on a pair of straw sandals. He stops to listen to the crisp sound of the falling rain, stretching out his hands to catch the raindrops.*

Huineng	(*Sings.*)
	The hounds you drove,
	To go after deer and doe;
	In caves and sheds of straw,
	To hunt was to live,
	A wild man in the mountains.
	They wanted to steal the *Dharma*,
	They wanted to hunt you down;
	Then like a bolt from the blue,
	You are honored and hailed,
	A teacher of Heaven and men.
	(*Huineng looks up and lets the rain fall on his face. Enter Yinzong in a hurry.*)
Yinzong	Master, what are you doing?
Huineng	Watching the rain and listening to my heart.
Yinzong	All the monks are gathered in the hall waiting for you to lecture them on the *Dharma*.
Huineng	Huineng has no *Dharma* to talk about. That which can be spoken is not the *Dharma*.

Yinzong   (*He waits patiently, his hands hanging by his side.*)
               You are the true successor of Buddha. Everybody is
               looking up to you. With due respect, I must insist on the
               Master's exposition so that all present will be
               enlightened!

Huineng   Huineng is unworthy of your respect and your
               compliments. I'm afraid that it'd be futile even if I spoke.

Yinzong   It all depends on one's *karma*. If the people are
               enlightened, then the merits will indeed be boundless.
               Master, please change into the *Dharma* robe you have
               inherited.

Huineng   *Dharma* robe or no *Dharma* robe, what is the difference?

Yinzong   If you had on an ordinary *kasaya* robe, you would be a
               mere lay brother, and only I would recognize your true
               identity. If you had on the *Dharma* robe, then everyone
               would know that you are the true inheritor of the *Dharma*.
               For the sake of the glory of the Buddhist order, and for
               the sake of the enlightenment of the deluded, I hereby
               request the Master to ascend the pulpit in the *Dharma*
               robe!

Huineng   Then Huineng will have no choice but to do that which
               he would not normally do. What indulgence! (*Bows and
               smiles.*)
               Please go in first. I will follow shortly.

               [*Yinzong smiles in approval. Exit. Bell tolls loudly. Exit
               Huineng.
               Enter the monks hurriedly one after another.
               Enter Yinzong. Bell tolling stops.*

Yinzong   Two hundred years ago in the Southern Dynasties, there
               was a tripitaka master by the name of True Meaning. He
               planted two *bodhi* trees on both sides of this pulpit. He
               also told his disciples to take good care of the trees, for
               later a Bodhisattva would come and perform the
               Supreme *Dharma* ceremony. We are really fortunate

today because this prophecy has come true. I welcome
to this pulpit Master Huineng, Bodhisattva-in-person
and true successor to the patriarchs. He will lecture us
on the teachings of the East Mountain Temple School.

[*Enter Huineng in Dharma robe.*

Huineng	(*Smiling.*)
	Let me sit under the tree here. The shade cools me. Greetings, everybody. Allow me to be honest with you. I don't know how to read. I can't understand the words in the sutra. If you want exegesis on the sutra, you should read the book yourselves. But I have one way to the *Dharma*, it has neither name nor words, neither eye nor ear, neither body nor concept, neither language nor manifestation, neither head nor tail, neither inside nor outside, nor anything in between, neither presence nor absence, neither cause nor effect, it neither comes nor goes, and it is not green, yellow, red, black or white. May I put the question to the learned members in the audience: what is this way?

[*The monks look at one another, afraid to answer the question. Shenhui, a young apprentice monk, stands up.*

Discipline Teacher	Young apprentice, what do you think you are doing?
Shenhui	I can't stand sitting down any more. My legs are numb.
Discipline Teacher	Then go away and do your work. Don't cause trouble here!
Huineng	Young people cannot sit still. Let him stand up. My way resides in the minds of everybody, but you have not been able to understand your mind and see your own nature. Let me hear what you have to say. (*Smiles.*) This way of mine has no rules.
Shenhui	Teacher, teacher, I have to pee!

Discipline Teacher	Watch what you're doing! You'll be punished for this!
Huineng	If you don't let the kid go he may burst. Go ahead, go.
	[*Exit Shenhui running. All are relieved and break out in laughter.*
Discipline Teacher	Quiet! Quiet! The lecture is in session! Be serious!
	[*Monks stop laughing out of fear.*
Huineng	It's serious, but it's also not serious. Mental state comes from the mind. If the mind is free, then it will be purified and beget wisdom. (*"Small drum" drum beat, imitating the clip clop of a running horse.*)
Discipline Teacher	What's the matter?
	(*Enter messenger from the prefecture government hurriedly, holding a horsewhip.*)
Messenger	His Excellency Prefect Wei Ju wishes to deliver this letter to the Grand Master Yinzong, Abbot of Dharma Nature Temple!
Yinzong	(*Rises to receive the letter. Finishes reading.*) Prefect Wei, the officers at the prefecture government and scholars from the four corners of the earth have learned that Master Huineng, true successor to the Buddha, has graced the county of Nanhai with his presence. Thereby an invitation has been extended to the Master to make accessible to all the door to the truth of the *Dharma*, to choose an auspicious hour and date to lecture on the Maha Prajnaparamita Sutra of the Mahayana School. On the same day let there be a magnificent ceremony, and let the pulpit be opened to receive all believers, encompassing monks or laymen, so that all the people will be delivered from their

	sufferings! The messenger is awaiting your reply by his horse. What, may I ask, is the Master's wish?
Huineng	It is my destiny that has brought me here. Let us choose a day so that we can combine the two lectures into one.
Yinzong	Messenger, please convey the Master's wish to Prefect Wei.

[*Exit Messenger. "Small drum" drum beat. Clip clop sound fades.*

Huineng	Let's call it a day. (*Stands up.*)
Yinzong	Let us all retire to our rooms to ponder on the question the Master has just asked. In this way his effort will not have been wasted and we will all benefit from his enlightening lecture.

[*The monks get up and look at one another. Exit. Enter Shenhui.*

Shenhui	What's this? It's all done? But I only went to pee! What did the monk talk about? What kind of *Dharma* is this?
Discipline Teacher	What do you think?
Shenhui	I knew it. If it wasn't the same old Buddha in the sutra, the stuff we've been chanting day in, day out?
Discipline Teacher	You garbage mouth! Hold your tongue! You've violated the rules of the temple. Give him a few smacks on the bottom! Master Huineng, do not spoil him!
Huineng	(*Yells.*) I've told you clearly that the *Dharma* has no name. How did you come up with a name?
Shenhui	The monk asked me, so I had to give it a name. If he hadn't asked about it, then it wouldn't have to have a name.
Huineng	(*Hits Shenhui with a club.*) Let me give you a thump with my club! Did you feel the pain?

Shenhui	Yes and no.
Huineng	Where was the pain?
Shenhui	My bottom.
Huineng	Where was there no pain?
Shenhui	The club.
Yinzong	Do not bother the Master any longer. Go! Go!
Huineng	What's his name, this naughty little kid?
Yinzong	His name is Shenhui. He has come here to learn the sutra and the disciplines. Let me ask him to leave the temple then.
Huineng	Let him stay. My feet are not well. Keep him by my side to look after me.
Yinzong	Holiness, where would you like to take up your residence?
Huineng	This temple is right next to the city centre. Whatever happens here, the officials will surely know about it. If I stay, the temple will lose its peace and quiet. I'm used to living in the mountains, so I think I'd better return there.
Yinzong	Does the Master have any specific place to go? I'll have to report to the Prefect on your whereabouts.
Huineng	After the *Dharma* gathering, I'll likely go back to the mountains in Caoxi in Shao Prefecture. I stayed there for some time before, it seems that I still need to be there to complete my destiny with the place.

[*Exit both. The faint ringing of a bell can be heard coming from backstage. Silhouette of the back of Boundless Treasure appears.*
Enter Singsong Girl amid music, singing from the orchestra pit downstage.

Singsong Girl	(*Sings.*)
	A beautiful body,
	A load of memories,
	A story hidden in the bottom of the heart,
	Only to recall but not to tell.

Boundless Treasure is you,
Boundless Treasure is me.
Walking, walking, keep on walking,
Who can understand the profound meaning?

[*Huineng is seen in the pulpit wearing the Dharma robe.
Silhouette of Boundless Treasure disappears. Enter Crowd.*

Huineng   (*Lectures.*)

Learned men and women!

All humans inherently possess the wisdom of *Bodhi
Prajna*, but due to the delusions in their minds, they fail
to achieve enlightenment by themselves.

As for my way to enlightenment, its aim is no thought,
its essence is no form, and its foundation no attachment.
What do we mean by no form? It is that when you are in
the world of forms, you are not attached to any form.

What do we mean by no thought? No thought means
you are not absorbed by any thoughts when you are
thinking.

And what do we mean by no attachment? No attachment
is in the self-nature of all humans.

Our thoughts should not have any attachments. If all
our thoughts, past, present and future, are linked
together without any interruption, then the *Dharmakaya*,
the essence body, will be able to detach itself from the
Rupakaya, the physical body.

When we are engaged in thinking, we should not be
attached to anything. Even if only one thought is
attached, all the others will be attached. This is known
as bondage. If we can be detached from all thoughts,
then we will not be burdened by any bondage.

Singsong Girl   (*Loudly.*)

This is the mystery of a Buddhist nun who is herself a
woman of mystery. Only a woman can solve it. But
women, every single one of them, all suffer from various

attachments of their own; they can't free themselves to solve the mystery. Then how can a monk, who is not a woman, be free to solve it?

(*Sings.*)

Sadness in the heart of love,
Entangling yet so refined;
Like a mist or a cloud,
It lingers and circles,
To puzzle and perplex;
And like a drizzle in the fog,
It can't be pushed away,
It can't be shoved along.
But can it ever be cut off?

Huineng Learned audience!

Maha Prajnaparamita are Sanskrit words. In the language of our nation they mean "great wisdom on the other shore." When one chooses to tread the path of enlightenment, one's *Dharma* body is the same as that of the Buddha.

Maha is "great." The mind's capacity is great, as great as that of the void. It encompasses the sun, the moon, the stars, the great earth, the mountains and rivers, all the myriad trees and plants, the good and the bad people, the good and the bad laws, and Heaven and Hell. They are all included in the void of "*Maha.*"

Human nature is the same; it is a void. All truths are but self-nature, which is revealed in humans as well as non-humans. One should not be attached to any truth, be it meritorious or otherwise. Earth, water, fire and air are the four *Mahabhutas*, or the four elements. They are but illusions and therefore belong to the void. The deluded only recite the *Dharma* with their mouths, the enlightened practice it with their heart!

Crowd (*Sing.*)

For great wisdom,
To the other shore!

	The four *Mahabhutas* are illusions,
	All is empty, all is void!
Singsong Girl	(*Loudly.*)
	Emptiness indeed! A woman, what will she be doing going to the other shore?
	(*Sings.*)

The myriad poses and alluring looks,
The unceasing wonderment,
The twists and turns,
The endless changes and mutations,
The pains inflicted on women,
How can a man understand? (*Exit.*)

Huineng   Learned audience, please listen carefully!

Troubles are the same as enlightenment. A deluded first thought, which clings to attachment, makes one an ordinary man; an enlightened second thought, which frees one from attachment, makes one a Buddha. Learned audience!

The wisdom of *Maha Prajnaparamita* is the most exalted, the highest, and the foremost. It is not attached to anything, not to the past, the present or the future, but all the Buddhas of the past, the present, and the future have attained and will attain their Buddhahood through its teachings. This great wisdom will guide us to the other shore and break up the troubles and defilements in the five *Skandhas*! Those who understand this *Dharma* will be free from thoughts, free from memories, and free from attachments. In this way, one is able to make use of wisdom to observe and to illuminate. At the same time, one does not need to take or leave any *Dharma*; he only has to realize his self-nature to become a Buddha. All sentient beings are Buddha!

Learned audience, chant after me!

Crowd   (*Sing.*)

Sentient beings are infinite in number,
We vow to deliver them all;

Troubles are infinite in number,
We vow to sever them all.
Troubles are no different from *Bodhi*,
All sentient beings are Buddha!

[*Enter Writer from one side of the stage. He stands and stops to listen.*

Huineng Learned audience!
We say that "sentient beings are infinite in number," and we say that "we vow to deliver them all." But I, Huineng, cannot accomplish the deliverance on your behalf, you must do it yourselves through your self-nature.
Within our physical body there are improprieties, troubles, foolishness, and delusions. We should deliver them by our innate awareness of propriety. Together with *Prajna* Wisdom, this enlightenment will remove ignorance and delusions, so that each of the sentient beings will be able to deliver themselves.
We say that "Troubles are infinite in number," and we say that "we vow to sever them all." This means that we should remove the illusions and fallacies from our mind, thereby obtaining self-enlightenment and Buddhahood. Buddha is all sentient beings; all sentient beings are Buddha.
(*Clasps his palms.*)

Crowd (*Chant.*)
Shanzai! It is good!
Shanzai! It is good!

Huineng (*Stretching out his hands.*)
Let me teach you all the disciplinary rules of formless-ness.
(*Goes down the pulpit and walks about among the crowd to teach them.*)

Crowd (*Sing.*)
All sentient beings are Buddha,

Buddha is us.

[*Exit Crowd, their head lowered. Writer moves forward.*

Writer	Master, can you teach me too?
Huineng	Teach you what?
	(*Writer draws a circle on his head with his hand.*)
Huineng	Sinner! Come back some other day.
Writer	Where can I find you?
Huineng	If you really want to find me, you'll know where to find me. (*Exit laughing.*)

[*Enter Singsong Girl again amid music.*

Writer	Lady, what kind of songs can you sing for me?
Singsong Girl	I'm here to entertain. What else can I sing about other than love, romance, boy-meets-girl, or things like that? Just tell me what you want to hear and I'll sing it for you. Mister, are you in a hurry to go to the capital for the civil examination? Or are you one of those talented scholars longing for recognition?
Writer	I'm doing nothing at present, just spending my life playing games. But I can't really get myself to sever my ties with the world either. I'm still a man of the world. Let me see. Why don't you sing "Snow in August"?
Singsong Girl	Mister, is there snow in August?

[*Zither music halts abruptly. Exit both Writer and Singsong Girl.*

Act II Scene 4

In Which the Patriarch Passes Away

["*Small drum*" *(for marking time) is beaten twice. Enter two guards.*]

Guard   Where is the abbot of the temple?

[*Enter Fahai with four monks.*]

Fahai   Who is it that dares to barge in here? Don't you know that the temple is a place of quietude?

[*Enter Head Guard.*]

Head Guard   Make way for General Xue Jian, eunuch of the Imperial Palace!

[*Enter Xue Jian and a guard.*]

Fahai   I'm Fahai. I must apologize for not welcoming you at the front door!

Xue Jian   His Majesty has handed down an imperial edict. In great haste, I have come from the capital, traveling day and night without tarrying. Please send for Master Huineng on the instant so that he may receive His Majesty's edict.

Fahai   Amitahba! Go call Master Huineng! Quick!

Monks	(*Passing on the word from one to another.*)
	An Imperial edict!
	Goodness gracious! Something big has happened!
	Tell the Grand Master to come at once!

[*Exit one of the monks, running.*

Fahai	May I ask the general to enter the guest chamber to change and take a bath?
Xue Jian	There is no need.
Fahai	For years I have been serving the master on the mountain, therefore I have no knowledge of the protocol for receiving an imperial edict. I hope the general will expound it for me so that I can make preparations by burning incense sticks and make obeisance —

[*Enter Huineng holding a staff in his hand, helped along by a monk.*

Huineng	Please accept my deepest apology. I am unaware of the reason why the imperial court is involved and why your lordship had to undertake such an arduous journey. Please let me be enlightened.
Xue Jian	I am Xue Jian, eunuch of the imperial court. By order of the Empress Dowager Zetian and the His Majesty Zhongzong, you hereby are to receive the imperial edict!
Huineng	(*Clasps his palms to make obeisance and receives the imperial edict.*)
	Huineng has not learned to read or write, may I trouble the honorable eunuch to read out His Majesty's royal letter? I will listen attentively, so that I will know what crime I have committed!
Xue Jian	The excellent teachings of the Grand Master have traveled far and wide and are respected by both Heaven and men. Why should there be any crime? The Empress Dowager and His Majesty in the royal palace are full of

great admiration for the Grand Master and long for your presence, despite a distance of ten thousand miles. Therefore they have sent your humble servant to tender an invitation requesting the Grand Master's presence at the royal palace, where there will be a temple for your exclusive use. May I ask the Grand Master to make preparations and set off for the capital as soon as possible? Your humble servant will be your escort!

Huineng	I'm old and my feet are not well. I can't walk far.
Xue Jian	This matters not. We have brought along a steed for your use. The Grand Master doesn't even have to walk an inch, and there are post stations that will provide for and look after your needs. There's really nothing to worry about.
Huineng	I have a bad back. I can't ride horses.
Xue Jian	Then we'll use a carriage. We can carry you on and off the carriage. And the driver will look after everything.
Huineng	These old bones of mine, I'm afraid they'll end up all broken and cracked before I arrive at the capital and present myself to the Empress Dowager and His Majesty. I might even have to trouble His Majesty to pick up my scattered bones. This will not do! This will definitely not do!
Xue Jian	But I have orders to follow. How am I going to answer to His Majesty?
Huineng	I'm a poor man, I have nothing in my possession except this *kasaya* robe handed down to me by my teacher. Let me give it to you and trouble you to present it to the Empress Dowager and His Majesty. In this way, I can requite in part His Majesty's solicitude.
Xue Jian	It's His Majesty's wish to summon you, not your *kasaya* robe! What's the use of having the rags worn by a monk? This edict is in His Majesty's handwriting. Don't be rude and give him the snub! (*Xue Jian takes one step forward and puts his hand on his sword.*)

Huineng	(*Bends down.*)
	You want this?
Xue Jian	What?
Huineng	(*Sticks his head out.*)
	Just take it.
Xue Jian	Take what?
Huineng	This old monk's head!
Xue Jian	What's the meaning of this?
Huineng	Doesn't His Majesty want to have me? Just take it.
Xue Jian	His Majesty wants you to go to the palace and expound your teaching. He didn't say he wanted your head!
Huineng	Excellent! Excellent! His Majesty also wishes to be a merciful Buddha.
Xue Jian	His Majesty's benevolence is spread far and wide. He has funded the renovation of temples all over the country and donated money to provide for Buddhist monks. His merits embrace the whole of China. Don't be rude! Don't be indiscreet!
Huineng	These are not merits.
Xue Jian	Then where can merits be found?
Huineng	Building temples, almsgiving, and patronage are merely meritorious work. But true merits reside in the *Dharma* body, not in the field of merits itself. Realizing our nature is known as *gong*; equality and righteousness are known as *de.* Together they make up *gongde,* which means merits. In our heart, we should see Buddha nature; in our behavior, we should be respectful. In all our thoughts we should espouse equality and righteousness, then the merits will be full and abundant.
Xue Jian	I don't understand the Grand Master's words. Would you mind if I recited them word for word to His Majesty?
Huineng	Thus I have spoken. I have no other teachings to expound to His Majesty. When self-nature is deluded, Buddha is all sentient beings; when self-nature is enlightened, all sentient beings are Buddha. Compassion is Guanyin, the

Goddess of Mercy; equality and uprightness are *Maitreya*, the future Buddha. Abandon any thoughts of the good and the evil, and nature will then enter into the body of the heart, which will become peaceful and be in a state of perfect rest. Please beg forgiveness from the Empress Dowager and His Majesty on my behalf, for Huineng has to stay in the mountains to recuperate from his illness and to take care of the temple. Extend my thanks to His Majesty for his benevolence. (*Clasps his palms.*)

[*Xue Jian is silent. He retreats and exits.*

Monks   (*Chant.*)
Excellent, excellent!
(*Sing.*)
Even His Majesty the Emperor
Wants to be a merciful Buddha!
In this world of myriad phenomena,
It's Pure Land, Pure Land everywhere.
Why are we still fighting, you and I?
They keep soldiers and generals, tell us why.

[*Exit monks.*
Huineng turns, his back facing the audience. He walks to the depth of the stage, coughs, then exits.
The stage turns dark. In the dark, there is a dish of charcoal burning in front of the meditation bed.
Enter Huineng holding a staff. His other hand is holding the kasaya *robe. He coughs, throws the* kasaya *into the fire and pokes at the fire with the staff. The fire is burning more vigorously now, and it is reflected on his face.*
Enter Shenhui, now grown up, on the side. He stops and observes silently.

(*Huineng halts his coughing, turns.*)

Huineng	Is it the little apprentice who has returned?
Shenhui	Your disciple has been following the instructions of the Master and traveling all over the country. I have set foot in the forest and the groves of the north, and I also visited Master Shenxiu's temple.
Huineng	Why have you come back?
Shenhui	Master Shenxiu answered the Emperor's call and went to the capital. Now he is the Patriarch of the two capitals and Master Holiness of His Majesty. So your disciple decided to come back to serve you.
Huineng	What kind of things did you see over there?
Shenhui	How about Master yourself? What kind of things did you see?
Huineng	How dare you fool around in your old master's presence! (*Hits him three times with his staff.*) It hurts, doesn't it?
Shenhui	Now it hurts, now it doesn't. (*Giggles.*) Shenhui feels the hurt, but Buddha nature doesn't.
Huineng	Shenhui! Don't you try to be smart with me!
Shenhui	(*Lowers his head.*) Please forgive me. It was my fault.
Huineng	It is the same with me. Now I see it, now I don't.
Shenhui	(*Looks up.*) Allow me to ask why.
Huineng	If I look in front of me, I see self-nature, which is void and silent, but I don't see anything at the sides. There is no puzzlement inside or out. Is there anything else you do not understand? (*Shenhui makes obeisance.*)
Huineng	Summon all the people in the temple. I have something to tell everybody.

[*Exit Shenhui. Huineng, supported by his staff, climbs on the meditation bed and sits cross-legged.*
Bell tolls. Enter Fahai and monks.
Tolling stops. Enter Shenhui. He stands aside.

Fahai	What is the Master's wish?
Huineng	(*Stops coughing.*)
	Come forward, all of you. I will leave the world in this month of August. I came to this world of humans with nothing on me, and I will leave empty-handed, not taking anything away. As long as I can remove your doubts, as long as we are peaceful and happy, then I will be content. Do you have any more doubts? Ask me while there is still time.
Fahai	Old Master, please stop saying things like this. It saddens us all.

[*The monks either lower their heads or kneel down on their knees. Only Shenhui remains wooden and motionless.*

Huineng	Look up, all of you. Take a look at Shenhui. He is young, but he is not affected. What kind of Zen are you people cultivating? For whom are you grieving? Are you worried about me and where I will go after this? If I don't know where I'll be going I certainly would not have said goodbye to you. You know why you are crying? Because you don't know where I'll be going. You only see life and death, but why can't you see where there is no life and no death?
Fahai	(*Takes one step forward.*)
	Your disciple has one question, but I don't know if I should ask the Old Master.
Huineng	We can disregard even life and death. Nothing is prohibited in the temple of Zen. Let us have it.
Fahai	After the Master is gone ... (*Looks around.*) Who will inherit the robe and the *Dharma*?
Huineng	What's the use of holding on to the robe if there is no *Dharma*?
	Ever since the beginning, there has never been anything. The *kasaya* robe, like all things, is extraneous to the self. If someone takes the robe and almsbowl and stirs up

trouble, then our order will be destroyed. After I'm gone, there will be heresies that will wreak havoc everywhere. But there will also be people who will be willing to brace slanders, and willing to sacrifice their lives to promote the cause and the teachings of our order.

Fahai Please forgive my obtuseness. I still have one more question.

Huineng If the question is straight from the heart, why not?

Fahai When our master is alive, so is the *Dharma*. But when our master is gone, how can the people after you see the Buddha?

[*Silence.*

Huineng Let the people worry about their own affairs. You will do well to look after your own! I have already said all I wanted to say. I will say no more, except for this one last sentence. Listen well: Seek not the Buddha from outside your own nature; he who does is a big, big fool. Take care of yourselves!
(*He sits up straight, his eyes lowered.*)

[*Exit monks in silence.*
The staff by the side of the meditation bed falls. Huineng passes away quietly. Silver bells ring delicately like silk.
Enter Fahai, tiptoeing. Scenery in the depth of the stage turns white.

Fahai How very strange! Suddenly all the trees and plants on the mountain have turned white, and on such a hot day! Is this really snow in August?

[*The bells ring continuously. The stage turns dark all of a sudden.*

Neige et feu 雪與光   Gao Xingjian   54 × 52 cm   2000

Act III

In Which Pandemonium Reigns
in the Hall of Worship

[*Enter Singsong Girl and Writer from both sides downstage. Sound of string music.*

Singsong Girl (*Sings.*)
Snow in August,
What a strange sight —

[*Writer looks up at the sky, holding up his hands as if to catch snowflakes.*

Singsong Girl (*Sings*)
Cao Mountain, quiet and serene,
A shadow cavorts with the clean, crisp wind.

Writer (*Recites.*)
A woodcutter —

Singsong Girl (*Sings.*)
Look at the green grassland,
Seek out your thoughts;
On snowy mountain tops,
There is meaning for us to know.

Writer (*Recites.*)
Teacher of a generation!

Singsong Girl (*Sings.*)
Even insensate stones think of moving,
And try to send us a message.

Writer	(*Recites.*)
	A lifetime of hardship,
Singsong Girl	(*Sings.*)
	The way of Heaven,
	They say it's enlightenment,
	It's only a mass of nothingness.
Writer	(*Recites.*)
	Nothing but horseplay!
Singsong Girl	(*Plucks the strings, raises her head and sings loudly.*)
	Dhya — na! (*Lowers her head to listen.*)

[*Exit Writer and Singsong Girl.
The stage is lit up brightly; enter Zen masters one by one.
This Master and That Master come forward.*

This Master	How to become a Buddha?
That Master	This one, that one.
This Master	What do you mean "this one, that one"?
That Master	It's not this one, and it's not that one.
This Master	(*Hollers.*)
	Ho!
That Master	(*Hollers.*)
	Ha!

[*One Master and Another Master come forward.*

One Master	Where in the world is Buddha? Speak!
Another Master	Your reverence, under your feet!
	(*One Master looks at his feet.*)
Another Master	Flying!
One Master	Not on this side, and not on that side. Flying? What are you talking about?
	(*He remains motionless, looking straight ahead.*)

[*The two masters look at each other and laugh out loud.
Enter Quite Master and Nice Master. The latter is carrying a staff.*

Quite Master	Quick, tell me, what is Buddha?
Nice Master	(*Strikes once with his staff. Turns and smiles.*)
	Whatever gets hit is not it.
Quite Master	(*Smiles.*)
	Then why are you still hitting?

[*Nice Master is wordless. Quite Master clasps his palms. Right Master and Wrong Master come forward. The latter is holding a bowl in his hands.*

Right Master	(*Laughing.*) Does a dog have Buddha nature?
Wrong Master	Water is in the bowl, clouds are in the sky. (*Pours water on Right Master's head.*)
Right Master	(*Shocked.*)
	Why are you doing this?
Wrong Master	(*Giggling.*)
	No reason.

[*Right Master and Wrong Master move away in silence. Enter Writer.*

Old Master	Mister, where did you come from?
Writer	From back there.
Old Master	Where are you going?
Writer	(*Bends down, takes off his shoe and shows it to Old Master.*)
	The sole has fallen off.
Old Master	What do you want to do?
Writer	Would you have a cup of tea?
Old Master	You've come to the wrong place, mister!
Writer	The place is right, but I'm not sure if I can find any Bodhisattva here.
Old Master	(*Hits him with his staff.*)
	You meathead! Don't you know that this is a Zen temple, and we don't worship idols here? All the Bodhisattva statues have been destroyed. Why have you still come here?

Writer	All sentient beings are Buddha, are they not? You're looking at one of them!
Old Master	Ha ha! This one here must be a writer!
Writer	Outside there are lots of sentient beings. I'm not sure if they're all Bodhisattvas ...
Old Master	Learned audience, the house of Buddha provides deliverance for all sentient beings. Whoever wants to become a Bodhisattva, step right in!
	(*Enter Singsong Girl and Laymen. The latter are carrying bricks, hauling timber or lifting tree stumps. There is a lot of hustle and bustle.*)
Singsong Girl	(*Pulls the strings. Sings in a high voice.*)
	Dhya — na!
Layman A	(*Hauling timber and leading the chorus to sing.*)
	Good men and good women,
	Come to the hall and meditate!
Laymen	(*Sing in chorus.*)
	All sentient beings are Buddha,
	We are Buddha.
Layman B	(*Places bricks on the ground and uses them as stepping stones. Treads on one brick with each step he takes.*)
	To the other shore. The heart is devout, and the steps are strong and steady. Leave not even one footprint —
This Master	(*Takes the brick in front of Layman B, chops it into two halves with his hand, and then throws the halves away.*)
	Bad *karma*!
	[*Layman B goes back to carry bricks. This Master keeps on chopping them.*
Layman C	Is our master practicing kung-fu? How many do you chop in a day?
This Master	I see one, I chop one. (*Again chops a brick into two halves and drops them onto the ground.*)
Layman A	Does our master play with cats too?

This Master	I don't know how! (*Chops another brick into two halves, which go plop when they fall onto the ground.*)

[*Layman D brings a stump, stands on it, and raises his foot as if he were practicing kung-fu.*

Layman D	Heaven moves in strength, and the superior man strengthens himself tirelessly.
Nice Master	(*Strikes down stump with one hit.*) More bad *karma*!

[*Layman D falls down.*

That Master	(*Bends down.*) Can you get up by yourself?
Layman D	I twisted my ankle.
That Master	(*Walks away in big strides.*) It doesn't matter, as long as your heart is straight.

[*Layman E gets hold of a piece of rope and tries to climb up on it. Exit Layman A.*

Layman E	Your Holinesses, lend me your eyes. You see how strong my wrists are? What do you think, uh?
Layman F	(*Draws a big circle on the ground with a piece of chalk.*) Gentlemen, gentlemen, please get out of the way. You know what they say, men all strive to climb up to high places. But for me, I just want to have a place to stand on the ground.
Layman G	(*Standing on a tree stump.*) Human life is just like a game. If you want to play, you'll have to know how to do it right and how to have fun doing it. What's the meaning of all this? Who knows? (*Looks down.*)
Layman H	(*Wielding a bamboo stick and turning round in circles.*) What do you think? Are you the centre, or am I the

	centre? Everybody loves to play God! Who wants to be a mere plaything? Everybody, what do you think? Who is circling around whom?
Layman I	(*Shielding a bell with his hand and walking backward.*) Careful! Careful! (*He knocks down the stump and Layman G falls down.*) I told you to get out of the way! Didn't you hear me?
Layman B	(*Still crawling on the ground and arranging bricks.*) Are you ever going to stop? Your bell makes people nervous!

[*The sound of a gong is faintly heard.*

Old Master	Now what? I wonder who can that be?

[*A heavy banging on the gong. Enter Crazy Monk carrying a big gong. His entire face is painted gold.*

Crazy Monk	A living Bodhisattva has descended. He's touring the four corners of the world! (*His hands are waving and his feet are dancing.*) The Star of Fortune shines up above! Money and treasures for everyone! (*He hits the gong once, giggling like the Buddha himself.*)

[*Enter Old Woman.*

Old Woman	(*Claps and then rubs her hands.*) Goodness gracious, so very kind!
Crazy Master	(*As soon as he hits the gong, he performs "face changing," and his face turns from gold to white.*) A crazy old fool, always laughing out loud…. That's me, your crazy old monk! (*Opens his mouth and reveals a mouthful of gold teeth.*)
Singsong Girl	(*Plucks the strings, walks to centre stage and sings in a high voice.*)

	Dhyana!
Writer	What a beautiful sight!
Singsong Girl	(*Turns and smiles at him.*)
	What are you looking at?
Writer	He who looks will have a throbbing heart!
Singsong Girl	(*Sways her waist slightly.*)
	It is a dead heart that stops throbbing, isn't it?
Old Woman	I was like that many years ago. Now my teeth have all fallen out, and I can eat only porridge.
Old Master	Lady, I hope you're not here to beg for alms. You know, the monks here at the temple need your support …
Old Woman	You're old and you're a monk. Why are you still afraid of women?
Old Master	Old woman, hold your sharp tongue!
Old Woman	But I meant well! So what if I'm an old woman? Can't I come and pay my homage at the temple? I'm just here to join in the fun. Suppose I sang a song, then what? Do you think the Bodhisattvas would be scared away by my singing?
Old Master	Never mind. I'm hard of hearing and I can't see well.
Crazy Master	I'm a monk, but I eat meat and I drink. See, I'm what they call a "flower monk," totally uninhibited! What have you got? Come on, show me all you've got!
Singsong Girl	Sure I'm here to entertain, and I make money with my art. But listen, my looks are not for sale!
Crazy Master	So what if you sold your body? Remember Buddha is present even in any old and stinking body.
Singsong Girl	Okay, monk! Listen up! (*Plays the strings.*)
Old Woman	This crazy monk, I'm not sure if he's really crazy or just faking it.
Crazy Master	Reality is not real, falsity is not false. Real or false, where can we find the real spirit of Buddha?
Old Woman	You're crazy. You don't look like you have it!
Crazy Master	(*Giggling.*)
	Old woman, what are you talking about, having and not having?

Singsong Girl   (*Plucks strings in fast pace. Sings in high-pitched style.*)
Snow in August,
How strange it is,
Cao Mountain is quiet and serene,
A beautiful shadow
Cavorts with the clear and crisp wind.
Look at the snowy mountain top,
There is meaning for us to know.
In the green grassland,
A place to seek out your thoughts.
Look again,
Even insensate stones think of moving,
And try to send us a little message.
The way of Heaven,
They say it's enlightenment,
It is but one big mass of nothingness.

All Masters   (*Sing.*)
The ultimate *Dharma* is no *Dharma*,
The big merit needs no cultivation.

Crazy Master   (*Strikes the gong hard, then puts his hand on it to halt the sound.*)
The big sound has no sound!

One Master   Where did this wild cat come from?

Another Master   Your Reverence, what are you looking for?

[*Enter Layman A stealthily. He has something hidden inside his shirt. When he squeezes it, it cries out "meow."*
He tiptoes and sneaks around. When he squeezes "the thing" inside his shirt again, there is another cry of "meow."]

That Master   (*Hollers.*)
Bad *karma*!

Nice Master   Get out of here!
(*Nice Master gives Layman A a thump with his staff, and the latter scurries all over the stage to constant cat meowing. Again and again Nice Master keeps on hollering and thumping with*

his staff. Everybody chases around aimlessly amid sounds of the gong and ringing bells. Pandemonium ensues.)

Layman A   (*Running away.*)
Go get him! Don't let him get away! (*Exit running.*)

Singsong Girl   (*Plays strings and sings.*)
Dhya — na!

All Laymen   (*Sing in chorus.*)
All sentient beings are Buddha,
And Buddha is us.

[*Enter Layman A with a cat under his armpit, running.*

Layman A   Don't let the guy get away!

Crazy Master   That's the guy, the cat guy! (*Hits the gong and laughs out loud.*)

[*Layman A scurries around the stage. The cat keeps meowing. Everybody laughs.*

One Master   (*Suddenly starts hollering and runs.*)
Thief! Thief! Catch him!

Another Master   Cat or thief? Which one are we supposed to catch?

Right Master   (*Suddenly starts hollering and running.*)
Fire! Fire! The inner chamber is on fire! (*Exit running.*)

Wrong Master   Get him! Get that crazy firebug!

Quite Master   What did you say? Who set whose house on fire?

That Master   He who set the fire knows he's the one.

Singsong Girl   (*Plays the strings and sings.*)
Dhyana!

Writer   (*Recites loudly.*)
If you want to play, go ahead and play;
If you want to make noise, just make noise.
Your house is your castle, how can anyone stop you?

[*Enter a monk and a layman. One of them is pushing a drum and the other hitting it. Loud drumming.*

Enter Right Master running. He is holding a torch in his hand.

Right Master	Your Reverences, where's the chamber that's on fire?
Layman A	(*Hollers.*)
	Don't let the thief get away! (*Chases after Right Master.*)
Right Master	Fire, fire, fire! (*Scurries around the stage.*)
Layman A	Meow, meow, meow — (*Chases after Right Master around the stage.*)

[*Exit Right Master running.*

All Masters   (*Chase after Layman A and run around the stage after him. Sing in chorus.*)
No matter monk or layman,
We are all human,
Bodhisattvas are always true,
Each and every one.

[*Exit Layman A running.*

All Laymen   (*Sing in chorus.*)
You suffer and I suffer,
You live hard and I live hard.
If not we'd all be in vain,
And our lives not worth living.

[*Enter Right Master waving a torch.*

Right Master	Thief! Thief! Catch the thief! (*Runs all over the stage.*)
Crowd	(*Sing in chorus.*)
	O fire, fire, fire, fire!
	O fire, fire, fire —

[*Enter Layman A holding a cat and chases after Right Master. Exit Right Master running.*

Layman A	He set the fire and he cries: "Catch the thief." Just like a thief shouting: "Catch the thief!"

[*Meowing is heard all over the stage. All chase after Layman A.*

Crazy Master	That's him, the cat guy! (*Hits the gong and laughs out loud.*)
Crowd	Get him!
	Get him!
	Don't let him get away!
Layman A	I'd like to see how you're gonna find it! (*Puts down the cat. Exit running.*)
Crowd	(*Chasing after the cat.*)
	Meow — meow — meow — meow —

[*Enter Right Master running while holding a torch.*

Right Master	It's burning! It's burning! My house is burning down! (*Exit running, his mouth spitting fire.*)
Layman C	The fire burns the cat,
	And the cat runs away,
	People stomp their feet,
	On this blasted day!
Wrong Master	Is this the trick you have in store?
	How can you get to the other shore?
Old Master	Amitabha! (*Exit.*)
Singsong Girl	(*Sings loudly.*)
	Dhya — na!
All Masters and Laymen	(*Sing.*)
	You're crazy, I'm crazy,
	You're crazy, I'm crazy.
	Small craziness is just not having it,
	Big craziness reveals the true spirit!
Crowd	(*Enter Layman A carrying a package wrapped in cloth.*)
	(*Shout one after another.*)
	Catch him!

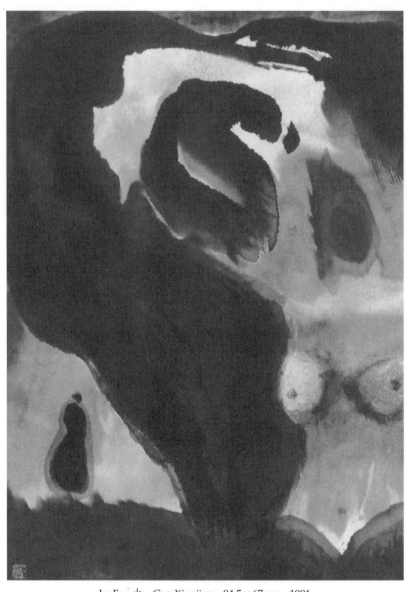

Le Feu 火   Gao Xingjian   94.5 × 67 cm   1991

Stop him!
Block his way!
Close him off!
Don't let the guy get away!

[*All, standing all over the stage, surround Layman A. Enter Old Master and Big Master, who is holding a big axe.*

Old Master   (*Pointing at Layman A.*)
That scumbag started it all! It's all his fault!
Big Master   What's going on here?
Layman A   (*Giggling.*)
The cat started it all, all by itself —
Big Master   Bring it over here!

[*Layman A hands over the cloth package. Big Master takes it and holds it steady on a stump and chops it with his axe in one go. Silence. Crowd disperse. Enter Right Master carrying an unlit torch.*

Right Master   It's all over.
Big Master   What's all over?

[*Silence. Fire gradually rises upstage.*

Big Master   Go! Go! Go! The worship hall has become a mad playhouse. This is no place to linger. Go away and make your own living! (*Exit.*)
Singsong Girl   (*Plays the strings and sings.*)
Dhya — na!
All Masters   (*Sing in chorus.*)
Great wisdom is to reach the other shore,
Great mercy is to have an ordinary heart.
All Laymen   (*Sing in chorus.*)
The brick carriers carry the bricks,
The cleaners do the cleaning up.

[*Everybody cleans up the stage while singing. Among them, one laughs out loud, one cries endlessly, one waves his hand, and one keeps on staring. Singsong Girl walks towards front stage, swaying her body.*]

Singsong Girl (*Sings.*)
The writer pushes his pen,
The butcher holds his cleaver.
In health you enjoy a cup of tea,
In sickness the drugs administer.

Writer (*Comes forward and sings.*)
The baker kneads his dough,
The sewage collector wakes up early.

Singsong Girl (*Sings.*)
The baby cries,

Writer (*Sings.*)
It's born.

Singsong Girl (*Sings.*)
The old man noiselessly

Writer (*Sings.*)
Passes away.

Singsong Girl (*Sings.*)
The lights are turned on,
Like many guns cracking at the same time,

Writer (*Sings.*)
Cannons go "boom, boom,"
On the other side of the river.

All Masters (*Sing.*)
The dead are sleeping, they're not moving,

All Laymen (*Sing.*)
The living have to live, and live happily!

Writer (*Sings.*)
House buyers buy their houses,

Singsong Girl (*Sings.*)
Smile sellers sell their smiles.

All Laymen (*Sing.*)

	Pile drivers drive their piles every day,
All Masters	(*Sing.*)
	When old bridges crumble new ones are built.
Writer	(*Sings.*)
	The world was like this in the beginning,
Singsong Girl	(*Sings.*)
	Even if the Tai Mountain falls in a moment,
	Or the Jade Mountain refuses to die,
	People look for troubles themselves.
Writer	(*Sings.*)
	The night rain hits the banana leaves,
	When a light carriage passes by,
	The wind murmurs.
All Masters	(*Sing.*)
and Laymen	Tonight and tomorrow morning,
	It's the same, the same, just the same,
	Tonight and tomorrow morning,
	It's goin' to be wonderful just the same,
	Still wonderful just the same!

[*The end.*

Paris, November 1997

Présence 自在　Gao Xingjian　89 × 86 cm　1997

Notes

P. 1, line 1: *Snow in August*

Snow in August was first written in Chinese in 1997. Since then it has undergone several revisions. The script was first published in 2000 in Taipei (Lianjing Chubanshe 聯經出版社). Then a revised edition was included in *Gao Xingjian juzuo xuan* 高行健劇作選 (Selected plays by Gao Xingjian) (Hong Kong: Ming Pao Press, 2001). Gao also wrote an opera version, in which he added many songs, for the 2002 production in Taipei. The script of the opera version was published in *Performing Arts Journal*《台灣戲專學刊》, No. 5, December 2002, and in the program *August Snow* 八月雪 (Taipei: Council for Cultural Affairs, Executive Yuan, 2002). The source text of my translation is the 2001 version in *Gao Xingjian juzuo xuan*, which according to Gao Xingjian, is the latest version.

The literal translation of the title 八月雪 is "Snow in the eighth month of the lunar calendar." Depending on the year, the eighth month of the lunar calendar usually falls in late August or September. Huineng died on the third day of the eighth month, when it was quite possibly still August in the Roman calendar. The time was still late summer in southern China, thus the peculiarity and unnaturalness of snow. I have translated 八月 as "August" because the weather in September in many parts of the world can be quite cool and snow is unusual but not unheard of, and "snow in September" would not be seen as strange as it is described in the play.

P. 1, line 8: Boundless Treasure 無盡藏

The literal meaning of Wujincang 無盡藏 is "repertory of boundless merits." Wujincang was also the name of a Buddhist nun. As recorded in *Xu biqiuni zhuan* 續比丘尼傳 (Biographies of Buddhist nuns, second volume) and other books, she once met Huineng when she was reciting the Nirvana Sutra and was surprised by the fact that he could clearly elucidate the tenets of the sutra despite his illiteracy.

P. 1, line 9: Hongren 弘忍 (602–675)

Tang Dynasty Zen master. It was said that he was a child prodigy. He met the Fourth Patriarch Daoxin when he was only seven and became a disciple. Later he succeeded Daoxin and was chosen as the Fifth Patriarch. His two most famous disciples were Huineng and Shenxiu. Huineng was the founder of the Southern School of Sudden Enlightenment and Shenxiu was the founder of the Northern School of Gradual Enlightenment.

P. 1, line 10: Shenxiu 神秀 (c. 606–706)

Tang Dynasty Zen master. When he was young, he studied the Confucian classics and prepared himself for the civil examination. (Some biographies say that he studied Daoism before joining the Buddhist order.) He probably became a monk around the age of fifteen. Later he went to see Hongren, who took him in as a disciple and made him First Instructor of the temple. After Hongren's death, Shenxiu left the temple and practiced Dhuta asceticism in his travels. As his fame spread, Empress Wu summoned him to the capital and bestowed on him the title of Abbot of the Two Capitals and Teacher of Three Kingdoms. He was known as the founder of the School of Gradual Enlightenment in Zen Buddhism.

P. 1, line 13: Yinzong 印宗 (627–713)

Tang Dynasty Zen master. He became a monk when he was very young and was a student of Hongren. An expert in the sutras, he was famous for writing a book entitled *Niepan* 涅盤 (Nirvana). The emperor once summoned him to serve at a temple in the capital city, but he refused. He met Huineng at Dharma Nature Temple and performed the ordination ceremony for him.

P. 1, line 14: Shenhui 神會 (c. 684–c. 758)

Tang Dynasty Zen master. When he was young he studied Confucianism and Daoiam before converting to Buddhism and becoming a monk at the age 40. (Some books claim that he was Huineng's "boy disciple" at age thirteen or fourteen, but scholars have proved this false.) A student of Huineng, he attacked the rival School of Gradual Enlightenment and was largely responsible for the revival and rise of Huineng's School of Sudden Enlightenment. Later he helped financed government troops in their campaign against the rebels during the An Lushan Rebellion. After the campaign, he was honored by the imperial court and given a temple at the capital to promulgate the teaching of the School of Sudden Enlightenment, which became the dominant force in Buddhism in China. He was known as the Seventh Patriarch of the Southern School of Zen Buddhism in China.

P. 1, line 17: Fahai 法海 (?–?)
Tang Dynasty Zen master. It was reported that he was immediately enlightened upon hearing Huineng's teaching of self-nature. There is not much information about his life, except that he was Huineng's disciple and he recorded the master's words which became *Tan jing* 壇經 (Platform Sutra). He also wrote a short preface to the book.

P. 3, 7th line from bottom: wooden fish 木魚
A percussion instrument made of a hollow wooden block, used by Buddhist monks and nuns to mark rhythm while chanting scriptures.

P. 3, 3rd line from bottom: *kasaya* 袈裟
A patchwork robe worn by a Buddhist monk or nun.

P. 4, line 14: Amitabha 阿彌陀佛
Amida Buddha (literally "boundless light") is the highest Buddha in the Western Heaven; also the Buddha of infinite change and infinite life. As personification of mercy, compassion, wisdom and love, Ambitabha has become the supreme object of devotion and faith in the Pure Land Sects in China and Japan. The expression "Amitabha" is the abbreviated form of "Namah Amitabha" 南無阿彌陀佛, meaning "Hear us, O Amida Buddha."

P. 7, 4th line from bottom: *Bodhi* 菩提
Supreme wisdom or enlightenment, necessary for the attainment of Buddhahood.

P. 9, line 2: *Dharma* 法
The teaching of the Buddha. The Buddha taught people enlightenment, so *Dharma* often refers to the "Way" or "Path" to enlightenment.

P. 10, lines 16–17: Lankavatara Sutra 楞伽經
A major sutra of Mahayana Buddhism. In the Lankavatara Sutra, enlightenment is regarded in terms of intuitive realization where the only reality is "absolute mind."

P. 11, line 1: field of merits 福田
The "field" (place) where meritorious virtues are nurtured and developed; the accumulation of practices which lead to enlightenment.

P. 11, line 10: *prajna* 般若
Insight or wisdom. According to the Sandhinirmocana Sutra, there are three kinds of insights: insight into worldly truth, insight into ultimate truth, and insight into benefiting sentient beings.

P. 11, line 13: *gatha* 偈
A hymn or chant of Buddhist teaching, usually written in the form of a poem.

P. 11, line 18: Bodhidharma 達摩
The name is traditionally associated with the founder of Zen Buddhism in China. The Grand Master Bodhiharma went to China from India around the end of the fifth century or the beginning of the sixth century.

P. 20, line 1: *ksana* 念
A thought; thinking; a momentary sensation.

P. 20, 6th line from bottom: the other shore 彼岸
In Sanskrit, "the other shore" is *paramita*, the land of enlightenment in Buddhism. According to Buddhist belief, one is able to cross the river of life — from the shore of delusion and suffering to the other shore of enlightenment — by cultivating and perfecting the *paramita* virtues of generosity, morality, patience, vigor, concentration (or meditation) and wisdom.

P. 28, line 2:
Huiming was reported to be the first monk to be enlightened by Huineng on the truth of the *Dharma*.

P. 32, 4th line from bottom: Maha Parinirvana Sutra 大般涅槃經
Commonly called the Nirvana Sutra. This was said to have been delivered by Sakyamuni just before his death.

P. 34, 2nd line from bottom: *arhat* 羅漢
The saint or perfect man of Hinayana Buddhism; the famous disciples appointed to witness Buddha-truth and to save the world.

P. 35, line 12: Bodhisattva 菩薩
Enlightened being, who has compassion and fully altruistic intentions to deliver people from suffering.

P. 35, line 12: Mahasattva 摩訶薩
Great being with compassion and energy, who brings salvation to all living beings.

P. 36, line 9: *Dhuta* 頭陀
An ascetic practice to get rid of the trials of life in order to attain nirvana.

P. 41, last 3 lines:
When Huineng gave Shenhui the club, it was reputed to be the beginning of the practice of *"banghe"* 棒喝 (clubbing and shouting) in Zen Buddhism — the master hits his meditating disciple with a club to jolt him into sudden enlightenment.

P. 44, 7th line from bottom: the four *Mahabhutas* 四大
The four elements of which all things are made: earth, water, fire and air. They represent solid, liquid, heat and motion.

P. 45, 11th line from bottom: the five *Skandhas* 五陰
The five aggregates, accumulations, or substances; the components making up "sentient beings," especially human beings. The five *Skandhas* are form, feeling, perception, impulse and consciousness.

P. 49, line 10:
According to *Song Gaozeng Zhuan* 宋高僧傳 (Biographies of eminent monks compiled in the Song Dynasty), the Emperor, after hearing Xue Jian's account of Huineng's sermon, was very pleased. He commended Huineng for his efforts in spreading Buddhism in China and presented him with a Buddhist robe made with*"mona"* 磨衲 (an exquisite fabric from Korea) and a crystal almsbowl. He also ordered the local prefect to renovate Huineng's temple and renamed it Guo'en Temple (Temple of National Grace) in honor of the Zen master. *Snow in August* chooses to omit the

Emperor's benevolence and instead accentuates Huineng's aloofness and his giving the Emperor the snub with his sarcastic remarks.

P. 52, last line: Guanyin 觀音
The Goddess of Infinite Compassion and Mercy, the most popular bodhisattva in Buddhism. She works towards the salvation of all.

P. 53, line 1: *Maitreya* 彌勒
Maitreya, meaning benevolent, is the bodhisattva who will appear in this world to become the next Buddha. In a Buddhist temple, his image is usually found in the hall of the four guardians facing outward, where he is represented as the fat laughing Buddha; in some places he appears as a tall Buddha.

P. 59, line 12:
"Cao Mountain, quiet and serene" is the semantic translation of the name of the Zen master Caoshan Benji 曹山本寂 (840–901).

P. 59, lines 17–18:
"… the green grassland,/ Seek out your thoughts" is the semantic translation of the name of the Zen master Qingyuan Xingsi 青原行思 (?–740). (Qingyuan Xunsi 青原尋思 in the play.)

P. 59, lines 19–20:
"On snowy mountain tops,/ There is meaning for us to know" is the semantic translation of the Zen master Xuefeng Yicun 雪峰義存 (822–908). (Xuefeng Cunyi 雪峰存義 in the play.)

P. 59, 2nd line from bottom:
"Even insensate stones think of moving" is the semantic translation of the Zen master Shitou Xiqian 石頭希遷 (716–790).

P. 60, lines 4–5:
"The way of Heaven,/ They say it's enlightenment" is the semantic translation of the Zen master Tianhuang Wudao 天皇悟道 (748–807). (Huangtian Wudao 皇天悟道 in the play.)

Pp. 59–60:

Qingyuan Xingsi was Huineng's disciple, and the rest of the Zen masters were pupils of his disciples, some of them several generations removed. In the play, some Chinese characters in the names have been changed to make them semantically meaningful. Others have their orders shifted. I have translated the names semantically after consulting with Gao Xingjian.

P. 60, line 10: Dhyana 禪那

"Chan" or "Zen", meaning meditation, thought and reflection, particularly abstract contemplation. Here it is used to invoke the name of Zen.

P. 64, 7th line from bottom: "face changing"

A technique in Sichuan opera which sees an actor changing face masks in quick succession.

P. 71, lines 13–15:

The source for this scene comes from a *koan* case recorded in *Wu Deng Hui Yuan* 五燈 會元 (Five lights combined). The story goes that during the reign of Emperor Dezong 德宗 in the Tang Dynasty, the monks of two houses in Puyuan 普願 Temple in Chizhou 池州 are fighting for the possession of a cat. The abbot, by the name of Nanquan 南泉, picked up the cat and asks the monks if they understand the meaning of the Truth. When none of them can provide an answer to the question, the abbot instantly cuts up the cat into two pieces with a chopper. Later a monk named Zhaozhou 趙州 returns to the temple. Upon hearing the abbot's question, he immediately takes off his shoes and places them on his head. The abbot sighs, "If you were here when I asked the question, the cat's life would have been saved!"

P. 73, line 7: Tai Mountain 泰山

A mountain in Shandong Province. One of the five sacred mountains in China.

P. 73, line 8: Jade Mountain 玉山

According to *Shanhai jing* 山海經 (Classic of mountains and seas), Jade Mountain is a mountain in the West. It has voluminous jade deposit in it and is the place where the Queen Mother of the West resides. Other sources say that Jade Mountain is not an actual mountain but a metaphor to describe someone with a handsome appearance. The phrase "the collapse of Jade Mountain" is used when someone is drunk and falls to the ground.